BORN FOR THIS!
Submission

Understanding Your Position as A Wife, Holy Submitted for GOD's Glory

Understanding Your Position as A Wife, Holy Submitted for GOD's Glory

Authored By LaShawna Thomas

BORN FOR THIS! SUBMISSION Understanding Your Position as A Wife, Holy Submitted for GOD's Glory

Copyright © 2021 by LASHAWNA THOMAS

Unless otherwise noted, Scripture quotations are from The Amplified Bible, Old Testament Copyright©1965, 1987 by the Zondervan Corporation. The Amplified New Testament Copyright © 1958, 1987 by the Lockman Foundation. Used by permission. Quotations identified as NIV are from The Holy Bible, New International Version®, NIV® Copyright ©1973, 1978, 1984, 2011 by Biblica, Inc.® Used by permission. All rights reserved worldwide. Quotation identified HCSB are from the Holman Christian Standard Bible®, Copyright © 1999, 2000, 2002, 2003, 2009 by Holman Bible Publishers. Quotations identified as NLT are from The *Holy Bible,* New Living Translation, copyright ©1996, 2004, 2007. Used by permission of Tyndale House Publishers, Inc., Carol Stream, Illinois 60188. All Rights Reserved. Quotations identified as BSB are from the Berean Study Bible (BSB) © 2016 by Bible Hub and Berean Bible

Used by Permission. All rights Reserved. Quotations identified as KJV are from the Holman KJV Study Bible Copyright ©2012 By Holman Bible Publishers Nashville, Tennessee. All Rights Reserved Quotations identified as KJV are from Bible Study Notes, King's English Glossary, and KJV Bible Concordance Copyright © 2012 by Holman Bible Publishers Nashville, Tennessee. All Rights Reserved. Quotation labeled Aramaic Bible in Plain English is from the Original Aramaic New Testament in Plain English-with Psalms & Proverbs Copyright © 2007; 8th edition Copyright © 2013 All rights reserved. Used by Permission.

This book and parts thereof may not be reproduced in any form, stored in a retrieval system, or transmitted in any form by any means - electronic, mechanical, photocopy, recording, or otherwise – without prior written permission of the publisher, except as provided by United States of America copyright law.

Inside cover picture: pxhere.com Mohamed Hassan

The examples and characters presented in this book are based on the author's actual life events throughout the years. The orientation, identities and names have been changed to protect the innocent. Any resemblance is coincidental.

ISBN: 978-0-9778348-9-1

Dedication

This book is dedicated to some very amazing people that played an integral role in the writing and completion of this work. First and foremost, I thank The Most High, God Almighty, My LORD and Savior Jesus Christ, and the Holy Spirit. I am nothing without You and I am so grateful You gave me the opportunity to place pen to paper. Shout out to my wonderful husband, my lover, my king, my very best friend, James. You have always been my biggest supporter and motivator; I would not have completed this without you pushing me to do so. THANK YOU! To the wonderful marriage relationships in my life, showing me that marriage is what you make it, and it can be absolutely beautiful! First, to my wonderful parents, James and Zina Dotson, who taught me that family comes first, and we must stick together like white on rice! To my grandparents, Gable and Gloria Searcy whose love and legacy is forever being written on my heart, Sophia and Eddie Boyce, your support was more than I could have ever expected, and last but certainly not least, Richa and Rodney Hood for your support and encouragement.

Preface

  There are so many opportunities to engage women around the topic of submission, so I take it as an honor to be able to share this forward to my sister my mentee my friend LaShawna Thomas. As I read the book, I thought about my own journey with the battle of what it means to be a submitted wife. The words were literally coming off the pages as I read. As a new wife, I struggled with submission because of the misrepresentation of what it was meant to be by bitter women who failed to honor their husbands. It was not until the 2nd marriage that I understood the true meaning of what a Proverbs 31 woman was and how submission is honorable.

  LaShawna is a writer who has lived experiences to match her passion for breakthroughs in others. The readers will be awakened in areas that were dormant and unhealed. As you read, keep your journal near and write out the simple prayers that will chart your new territory. This book reminded me of what a journey it has been to embrace the purpose of my life. Our purpose is to fulfill what God had in mind when he created me in His image and likeness. As you open this book my prayer for you is that you will come to the end of your journey of battling what it means to be submissive. May you embrace all that God has for you and fall into the freedom and the liberty of God, using submission as a tool for a productive life.

  LaShawna has not only given us the keys from the word of God she shares her experiences, her frustrations, her journey and her triumph. When we understand that we relate to one another through relationship and that each of us have a part to play in the relationship

  We will trust God's intended purpose for us. God purposed us from the beginning of time. From your mother's womb there was a plan and an assignment for your life. There was a way of being that God created in your existence and that will never be changed. As you read this book, I would invite you to open your heart, mind and your spirit to receive your assignment for this new season. The book is calling you to understand whose you are and understand how you can build a life that is full of joy, prosperity and wholeness in alignment with what God's plans and purposes are for your life. LaShawna thank you for this gift. Thank you for being an example of the proverbs 31 woman. Thank you for being open and sharing your own story that it might be light to others. I speak over you even greater breakthrough and deliverance as you continue to soar and to put pen to paper and books to come. God bless you!

    Kelly Ramsey, your friend and Sister

Words of Praise and Wisdom

Wow! I am so amazed and proud of my beautiful, divinely anointed gift, my good thing. I promise you, every one that reads the pages of this time fitted book will be eternally blessed by the inserts and display of this great woman of GOD Almighty's golden heart. Submission is key to the unlocking and the fulfilment of our hearts to receive GOD Almighty's heart of fulfilment of fruitfulness. This ensures the fullness of pleasure and goodness with your spouse through GOD Almighty's plan. Submission, if you will, is the measure of delightful indulgence that compliments the building of endurance giving each spouse a sense of fulfilment to enter and obtain obedience aligning ourselves to be brought to and brought forth in our relationships.

James Thomas, *Loving husband of LaShawna Thomas and Father to their beautiful children, Pastor of House of HIS Dwelling Ministries, Conyers, GA*

Marriage is a bond between two people that should not let anyone, or anything come between it. Always be faithful, honest and communicate to one another. Marriage is like a rubber band, you can always stretch it, but it will come back together!

Zina Dotson, *Beautiful and sweet mother of LaShawna Thomas, wife of 35 years to James Dotson, a loving mother, and grandmother*

TABLE OF CONTENTS

INTRODUCTION 12

CHAPTER 1. SUBMISSIVE WHILE BEING PRODUCTIVE 15

CHAPTER 2. WHAT IS SUBMISSION 32

CHAPTER 3. REAL JOY 47

CHAPTER 4. I AM A PROVERBS 31 WOMAN 58

CHAPTER 5. MY TESTIMONY 65

CHAPTER 6. IT BRINGS REST AND PEACE 73

CHAPTER 7. PRAYER FOR SELF AND SPOUSE 85

ABOUT THE AUTHOR 90

Introduction

"We are assured and know that [GOD being a partner in their labor] all things work together and are [fitting into a plan] for good to and for those who love GOD and are called according to HIS design and purpose." Romans 8.28 (AMPC)

We are not alone. GOD is always right here with us to help us in every area of our lives. This includes the area of submission. HE literally partners with us, just as the Scripture in Romans 8.28 tells us, in our work of life for everything to be good. Regardless of what the situation may look like, it all comes together to fit into HIS perfect plan for our lives. We must have faith in knowing that the plan and the purpose is good. Too often we get stuck on the not knowing or the negative outcomes of our circumstances, rather than submitting to HIS will and trusting in HIS promises that are written in HIS holy word. I encourage you, as you read through the pages of this book, that you truly take the opportunity to pray and ask HOLY Spirit to help you learn how to submit to HIM in every area of your life. Pray that your eyes are opened to understand what submission should look like in the life of a Believer, as a child of GOD Almighty.

"In the same way, you wives, be submissive to your own husbands [subordinate, not as inferior, but out of respect for the responsibilities entrusted to husbands and their accountability to GOD, and so partnering with them] so that even if some do not obey the word [of GOD], they may be won over [to Christ] without discussion by the godly lives of their wives, when they see your modest and respectful behavior [together with your devotion and appreciation - love your husband, encourage him and enjoy him as a blessing from God]".1 Peter 3.1-2 (AMP)

Take time to read that Scripture again. It is the foundation for this book. We as wives are told to be submissive to our own husbands, not because we are inferior in any way, but out of respect for the responsibilities GOD gave him as a husband. Now I know some may be reading and thinking, my husband doesn't deserve my submission because he is not taking his responsibility as a godly man. However, the Scripture covers that as well. Honestly, the behavior, attitudes, and actions of our husbands are no excuse for us not to submit to them and do as the Word of GOD tells us. Read the Scripture again, slowly, and take time to grasp every word that is being stated. Our husbands are a blessing from GOD, and we should treat them as such. They are not distractions, hindrances, or mistakes. Our reasons for getting married often get misconstrued once the honeymoon is over because life starts to set in. It is no longer the beautiful wedding gown, handsome tuxedo, fancy food and hotel room. The bells and whistles are gone, here comes the bills and responsibilities. However, the honeymoon does not have to be over just because life begins. Life should be the reason the honeymoon phase never ends. A marriage full of submission is a marriage full of blessings, blessings from GOD Almighty. Those blessings include love, joy, peace, encouragement, and companionship. You will find that you have favor not only with GOD but with man as well.

**Please note in this book, I refer to GOD (I AM; I AM THAT I AM, Exodus 3.14) as GOD, GOD Almighty, The Most High, and GOD Most High, the Living GOD, the One and Only True and Living GOD, Father, Heavenly Father, and Yahweh and use these names interchangeably. I reference Jesus Christ as the Son, the Son of the Living GOD, the LORD, and Savior. I believe these are all attributes of The Most High and are One in the same. The Most High is GOD the Father, GOD the Son (Jesus Christ) and GOD the Holy Ghost (Holy Spirit). THEY are all One and have Their Own unique attributes as well. Our Heavenly Father sent His Son Jesus the Christ to earth to die for our sins and by the power of His Holy Ghost (Holy Spirit), raised Jesus from the dead, and He is alive today. I want to express this to eliminate any confusion that may arise while reading this material. I am not referring to any other 'god' or 'gods' when I use these names. His name is I AM and He is The Most High, the One and Only True and Living GOD.

I pray that as you read the pages of this book, you will get a life changing experience that will bring hope, confidence and change to your marriage. The events that happened in my marriage are nothing uncommon and you will more than likely find yourself in the pages as you go through it. My hope is that you will have a new perspective on submission in marriage or at least gain more insight, so that your relationship can be further fulfilled and reflect the love of Christ in every area.

I also hope to answer the question of what a successful marriage should look like in the eyes of The Most High, according to His Word. A successful marriage reflects the covenant between Christ and the church in the flesh. As you read through the chapters of this book, my prayer is that you will gain some understanding of how our marriage relationship should be an outward expression of that covenant and how our role as wives play a significant part in the success of it. This book is geared toward women, wives specifically, but I do believe that unmarried women, men, and husbands will benefit from the information and my testimony that will be shared.
GOD bless you.

LaShawna

Chapter 1
Submissive While Being Productive

Productive:

1) Having the quality or power of producing especially in abundance
2) Effective in bringing about
3) a. Yielding results, benefits, or profits
   b. Yielding or devoted to the satisfaction or the creation of utilities.
4) Continuing to be used in the formation of new words or constructions
5) Raising mucus or sputum (as from the bronchi) -a productive cough

Any successful marriage takes work. Unfortunately, as women, I do not think most of us believe that submission is part of that work. We must work to not only be respectful but also submissive to our husbands as we are to the Lord. But what does a successful marriage look like? Some of us wives hear the word submit and cringe at the thought of having someone 'lord' over us, telling us what to do, as if we need another daddy. And let's not talk about respect, too many times we have had the mindset of "I'll give respect when I get respect." These thoughts are all too familiar because that was me! The very moment my husband James even attempted to tell me what to do, especially if I was already in a mood, my mindset was immediately defensive and screaming, 'YOU ARE NOT MY DADDY, DON'T TELL ME WHAT TO DO!' Then I start asking myself questions and answering them. 'Does he really expect me to listen to him and do things his way when he doesn't even give me the same respect?! I don't think so! Got me confused with somebody else. Did he forget who he was talking to? He must have because he is dealing with the wrong one. I mean really, who does he think I am? His servant! Not today, I don't think so!' I see you doing the head-neck roll as you read those last few sentences!

These are the very attitudes that we must guard ourselves against to truly live a marriage that reflects the GOD-given covenant that He ordained from the very beginning of time. The Scriptures tell us in Ephesians 5.24 that wives are to submit to their husbands in everything! Going on to say that we are to respect and revere them, notice him, regard him, prefer him, esteem him, praise him, love, and admire him exceedingly! (Ephesians 5.33 AMPC) Being a wife is hard work and that job is even harder when we have a spouse that does not have the same ideals of what a marriage should look like.

As you noticed, I started this chapter with the Merriam-Webster Dictionary's definition of *productive*. I started with the definition because I believe every way this word is defined pertains to marriage and the work necessary to be successful, right down to the sputum! I will use these definitions as the basis for this chapter. To be submissive while being productive refers to the work it takes to have a successful marriage with a foundation on Jesus Christ.

We have all heard it said that marriage takes work, and well, it does! Anything we really want in life we work for it. We go to college to obtain degrees, attend trade school to learn new skills and join the workforce, and we go to basic training to prepare for the military. No matter the avenues we choose to take for our professional lives and our careers, we work, and we work hard to get there. Sometimes becoming so consumed in a thing, it encompasses our very being until we feel we have accomplished the goal. Yes, marriage takes a lot of work, and that work must be productive for it to be successful. So, the question I pose is, why do we work so hard for so many things, but when it comes to our marriage relationships, not so much? I believe the answer lies in the mistaken idea that once we get married, we do not have to do anything to stay married. There is even the truth in knowing that before getting married, there should be a level of investment made to understand our roles and responsibilities as wives. Just like the years of study needed to get that college degree, we need to take time and learn what it means to be a "good thing" (Proverbs 18.22). We should learn not only how to be submissive and respectful to our husbands, but also know who we are as an individual, and as a daughter of The Most High.

For some women, the thought of being submissive looks like being a doormat for a husband to walk on and over, day in and day out. It's losing sight of who we are as an individual and allowing the husband to 'run amok' however he pleases. But this is so far from the truth! The fact of the matter is, it takes a strong willed and determined woman of GOD to be truly submissive and be genuinely good at it. Submissiveness is a quality of character and a power! When done productively in our marriage relationships, we find an abundance of blessings. Effective submissiveness will help you to listen to your man, explain your needs and wants, and both of you get what is best for the relationship. Honestly, only a woman who is first submitted to The Most High can submit to her man, respect him and love him, take care of the home, the children, go to work and/or school, nurture your entire self being and still look good while doing it. Its productivity as its finest, and we can make it look effortless.

Still, we as wives find ourselves in a season of our lives, where this is not evident. We find it so easy to submit to our jobs by doing the work assigned to us, or to the leadership at church being good servants, but submission in marriage is like saying a curse word! Why is that? Society has wrongly led us to believe that submission in marriage is a sign of weakness, it is being the victim and not the victor. It is being controlled instead of taking control. Submission is not dominance.

We also must come to a place in a society where it is becoming more and more common for the man to stay home and be with the children while the woman goes out to work. It is also not uncommon to find when both husband and wife are employed, the wife makes more money than the husband. This role reversal has brought on the belief that women can do whatever men can do, including taking on the role as head of household. Please stay with me here. I am not saying the women can't do what men can do or make it appear as though women are less than men in any way. What I am saying is that God Most High gave men and women specific roles because of how he made us, and our world today has thwarted those roles to fit personal ideals and beliefs. If we truly take time to look at certain job roles, most women would not be doing certain positions because of our delicate nature. It is not to say that a woman COULD NOT do certain jobs, but we all know that SOME work is truly done better by a man. It's just how GOD Most High designed us. I know many would disagree with me here and that is fine, we all have a right to our opinion. That is not an insult and that is not because you are not as 'strong' as a man. GOD Most High made us differently, and our strength was given to us in different ways. A woman could not ever gain the muscle capacity that a man could because He chose to design us in a way that compliments the man, not competes with him. Just like a man will never be able to carry a child because that would go against the plans and purposes of The Most High. The inability for a man to carry a child is not an insult nor does it make the man less important, it is just the way HE designed HIS people.

I know for myself that I would not take on the job position of being a professional tree logger because I feel that is a position where a man could be more beneficial in tearing down huge trees. Now if it is the difference between my family being protected from the cold and staying warm in the winter, and push came to shove, I would go and chop down a tree to provide wood for my family. Is this to say that women cannot be loggers, of course not! There are women in that field that love their jobs and are thriving in this male dominated industry. With that being said, how many women do you know say I want to grow up to be a logger? I am sure there are not many, if any at all.

In the beginning, GOD Most High made man first and gave *him dominion.* Before Eve came into the picture, Adam was already working productively taking care of the garden and naming the creatures. His vision, assignment, and purpose were in full effect and Adam was successful. After naming all the cattle, birds, and beasts, it was then that GOD Most High decided Adam should not be alone. The *help meet* was then made from Adam's rib and brought to him for them to be joined as one. Eve was bone of his bone and flesh of his flesh. (See Genesis 2). GOD Most High ordained marriage as man being the head of the household (Ephesians 5.23); told them to love their wives just like Christ loved His bride, the church, dying for her, making her holy, cleansing her with the Word, to present her radiant, holy, and blameless; loving his wife so much, as though she is his very own body. That is a tall order to fill. Wives, you need only to submit and respect. (Ephesians 5). GOD Almighty took His time to form and fashion you with such detail and splendor to be there to help your husband and compliment him and the vision that was given.

With The Most High's plan for family in effect, we have knowledge given in the Scriptures of the order of the family unit. As women it is an honor to take the position of wife and fulfill His plan and not our own. To be holy, blameless, radiant, and not have to do it alone is an amazing place to live.

Productivity is proactive, reactive, and consistent. We go to work every day, meeting quotas and deadlines, we use effective communication to help others, and we come up with strategies that ensure the best results (whether that be closing a sales deal, cleaning an office building, or overseeing employees); all of this to gain monetary compensation at the end of the pay cycle. We are productive daily. We do what is necessary to keep employment, daily. We stick to work related routines every day because we know we need money to pay our bills and take care of our families. The same time, effort, and productivity is necessary (even more important) in our marriages to ensure we get compensation for the energy taken for a successful marriage. I have heard it said once before that marriage is a business that includes two partners, with the same vision and passion to make it work. In some ways, I believe this to be true. But I genuinely believe that marriage is much more than just a business. Businesses fail and go bankrupt or merge with other businesses to stay afloat. GOD ordained marriages should not fail, go bankrupt and certainly should not be merging with other businesses to work it out!

    Marriage is a lifelong covenant that brings together two totally different people from different backgrounds and upbringings, with two separate visions, that have decided to bring those visions together to live out their GOD-given purpose as a union that cannot be broken by no one or nothing. Having the quality of submission, as a wife, is the power necessary to take on your husband's vision and see it to fruition while your vision is still in full force. That's right, woman! YOUR vision does not go away or get placed on the back burner. GOD Most High did not give you a vision to do nothing with it, and your husband should not, at any moment, make you feel like your vision has no purpose or is no longer valid once you are married. The same is true for his vision. You may feel that his vision is not as grandiose or important as yours, but that gives you no place to put his vision off as nothing or something that should be done later. Visions from GOD Most High, are just that -The Most High's Vision; we as mere creatives have no place to determine when or how a vision should come to pass. If YOU can make it happen, it's not from HIM anyway. Any vision from The Most High is not capable of being completed without HIS doing. Having the quality of submission is a powerful weapon The Most High gave every woman. When used effectively, it produces an abundance of life altering results. Results that yield great profit and gain. A happy life and holy union that is pleasing to The Most High. Your vision and his vision can both be accomplished as you work to fulfill the covenant vision that became established when you both said, "I do."

A proactive relationship will look for ways to be creative in every possible situation that encourages a godly response. For instance, when it comes to productive submission, I choose to honor my husband by praying for him daily and asking GOD to give him wisdom in all his daily tasks. When I do this, I am creating a space for The Most High to be the center of his decision making and therefore intervene when necessary, rather than waiting for him to mess up and then choosing to pray. Granted, we all make mistakes, however I believe in prayer, and I trust GOD Almighty is listening when I pray for James and his decision-making process. When we have a proactive mindset about our marriages, we prepare ourselves for the leading of The Most High in our walk of faith. Commit your ways to the Lord, trust in Him and He will do it. Psalms 37.5.

Prayer is one of the many godly habits we should have and one that should be consistent. Consistency in prayer brings us closer to GOD. When we have an intimate relationship with our Creator, we can then effectively give and show intimacy to our husbands. We should strive to pray alone and with our spouses every day. If you are in a place where you pray and your husband doesn't, don't stop praying. Keep going before the LORD on his behalf, interceding for him and asking GOD to prick his heart and give him a godly conviction to change. Please know that constantly telling, or "gently nudging" your spouse to pray, read the bible, go to church or any of those things can push him away. Eventually he will feel like you are nagging and/or complaining. We definitely want to encourage growth for the spiritual lives of husbands, but we don't want to completely drive them away in the process. Allow God to change him through your effective prayers. Pray the Word (Bible Scriptures) over him and watch GOD make the transformation.

Consistently walking and striving to possess the Fruit of the Spirit is another habit we should diligently work to have in our daily lives. Having the character of the Holy Spirit helps us to respond to every situation and circumstance we could face in a way that is pleasing to the Father. If something bad happens and our first reaction is to respond in love, we can find ourselves in a good place to gain insight, comfort, and real resolution. Our Heavenly Father does not want us to be lazy Christians and He certainly doesn't want to see our marriages fail. We must choose to be productive, it doesn't just happen. We don't go to work and then expect to be effective and meet our productivity quotas by just sitting at the desk. We must be aware of the tasks at hand, know the expectation and then do the work. That same mindset is vital to having an awesome marriage. Marriage is the work; what expectations do you have? What tasks need to be done to meet those expectations? Once we have it, it must be consistent and be adaptable to fit the needs of each other as we continue to grow in the grace and knowledge of GOD, as well as in our physical nature. You may have eaten chicken nuggets and mac and cheese when you got married all those years ago, but now you want steak and potatoes! Intimacy will keep you on point to grow with the changing needs of your spouse as well as for yourself.

Effective in bringing about.... Real submission in all its effectiveness brings about the fruit of the Spirit. It brings an inner sense of accomplishment and peace that comes only from GOD Almighty. Real love, real joy, real peace, real longsuffering, real meekness, real gentleness, real goodness, genuine faith, and true temperance (self-control). Truly, how can we exhibit and be effective in any of these traits without first submitting to the One who gave them? Possessing the fruit of the Spirit allows us to take on the very nature of GOD Most High Himself. The only way we can possess this Fruit is to be always led by the Holy Spirit and turn completely against the works of the flesh -being crucified with Christ (Galatians 5). The Most High created us to give Him glory, we were created for His good pleasure. The greatest way we can show our praise and give Him all the glory is by humble submission to Him and His will for our lives. When we truly submit to God Almighty, we can then submit to our spouses. His character makes submission easy. Submission to GOD Most High is reflective of the submission to our husbands.

Productive submission yield results that can only come from our willingness to honor our husbands in this way. When we are devoted to having submitted marriage relationships, we gain a satisfaction from it that can only be explained from a mindset that understands submission. The benefits are so rewarding when submissiveness is at work. Trust is built and you will breed and cultivate a peaceful, loving and encouraging environment, for yourself, your marriage, and your children. When true submissiveness is active, it will bring about a harmony between you and your husband. You will find it easier to have quality conversations (which all of us as women want) and amazing, sexy love sessions (which all our men want)! Seriously, there is nothing sexier than a strong-willed woman, who is not only able to stand her ground, but is also able to stand by her husband's side and give him the reins; trusting him, as he trusts the Lord, to lead you both into greatness. The satisfaction that comes is worth it!

In the early years of my marriage, James took it upon himself to make most of the decisions in the household, whether it was finances or what to eat for dinner. In times when he would ask my opinion on a matter, he would still make the decision based on how he saw it best (most of the time opposite of what I said). If, or should I say when, things didn't work out as planned, he would always come to me and expect us to come up with another solution.

"So you mean to tell me, YOU can make the decision, and YOU mess it up, then WE have to fix it?!" Trust me! It got old fast. However, doing it this way gave James the responsibility of operating as man of the house in that area, and eventually coming to realize that trying it my way was not an insult to his ideas or his way of doing things. I will admit that allowing my husband to make ALL the decisions was a challenge, especially when I clearly see that his way is going to be disastrous. But it was necessary (in my relationship) to show him that I trusted him enough to make decisions for our family. If things turned out badly, I also had to be mature enough to not walk in the 'I told you so' attitude. The 'I told you so' stance in any relationship can be hurtful and cause strain. James knew he messed up and he knows he should have done things differently, so he certainly doesn't need me throwing it back up in his face, reminding him of his failure. Unfortunately, this holds true for a lot of us wives when it comes to the man making decisions. Some of us won't even give our spouses an opportunity to decide out of fear that they will just mess things up. Or assume they don't know how to do it like you, and any other way just won't work. This is not healthy, and it is not productive in bringing about a relationship that honors God Almighty and our spouses. This is a prime opportunity to eat up that Fruit of Self Control and Meekness, leaning on the Holy Ghost for the strength to hold your peace!

Understand that if you can be submissive to a job and your friends and even your children, because let's face the facts of the matter; we compromise with our friends every time we make plans for dinner, movies or just hanging out. We work with our little children on what to wear to school, especially when they become old enough to decide what they like and don't like. Even submitting to allow our little princess to wear a lime green tank top and orange tutu because it looks pretty. How about allowing our little man to wear his superhero costume? EVERY. SINGLE. DAY. because we value his choice of expression. Besides, it's just a phase anyway and he will grow out of it! Some would say that this is just a form of compromise and not submission. That may be true in a sense, however, understand that (in the case of allowing children to wear what they want), there are some parents that will not allow their children to go out in that costume every day and will put the foot down, despite the tantrums and tears. Why, because we are the parents, we know what is best, and we expect our children to do what we know to be right. The Most High is the same; He knows what is best and has given us His written word (the Holy Bible) to follow and do what He says, because it is right. We don't stand before our Heavenly Father and negotiate on whether we can take the long way or the short way. It takes submission, not compromise to go the way He tells us, no matter the road. Of course, there are exceptions here and I certainly am not telling you to sit idly by while your husband makes decisions that could harm the well-being of your family. If there is a decision being considered that could be detrimental to the physical, mental, emotional, or even spiritual welfare of your home, then speak up! GOD Almighty would never put you or your family in a place where He would fail to take care of you, so we must ensure our decisions do the same.

Now regarding the part of the definition pertaining to raising mucus, when we catch a cold and have buildup of fluid and mucus on the inside, doctors and those in the medical field encourage coughing to help loosen the mucus. I recall a time when one of my children had an awfully bad cold that seemed to last a while, so I chose to take my child to the doctor. When advising the doctor that I was giving cough medicine because she had such a horrible cough, the doctor proceeded to tell me that the coughing was necessary for the fluids to break up and be released from the body. Cough suppressants hinder the body's natural response to relieve itself of the blockage. I felt the cough was making her miserable, so I wanted to soothe her. However, in my efforts to help my child get better, I was aiding in the prolonging of the cold, by preventing the cough!

How does this relate to submission, you may ask? Well, I fully believe that when there is a blockage in our marriage relationships, it's more than likely because of a lack of submission in some area. Dishonesty, miscommunication, hurt feelings, selfishness are the mucus and sputum. Submission is the cough that comes to release all that is working against the relationship. Lack of submission (for the husband and wife) will almost always breed a web of problems and issues that only get worse with time if not addressed properly. The more we suppress and try to block what is needed for healing, the harder it becomes to overcome. Just like a cold if left untreated can lead to worser symptoms and sickness, in a marriage if the issues continue to go unattended, it will take much more work to get through and experience healing. We also know that someone with a compromised immune system can experience even greater health risks if he/she were to catch a cold or get sick. In marriage, if it's already compromised, experiencing any type of difficulty, it will be an even greater blow if that marriage were to be struck with infidelity or abuse. Just like mucus from cold or allergies must come up and out for you to fully experience relief, we must address our marital woes and clear them out, at the first sign of trouble, to experience wholeness.

For the longest time, I would suppress my emotions to avoid confrontation with my husband. I got married at a young age and did not have any type of real advice or effective counseling prior to my marriage to help me gain understanding on how to deal with conflict. With that, when it came to arguments and disagreements, I did not handle them very well. I would suppress anger, fear, and hurt feelings for weeks and months at a time, until I could not keep them bottled in and I would just explode. The smallest offense would tip me over the edge and the explosion was so outrageous I would literally kick holes in the walls of our home, saying disrespectful and hurtful things. I was a fighter. I would scream and yell until I felt as though my point was made. This anger would last for days. Needless to say, this was very unhealthy and very unproductive for my relationship with my husband. It wasn't until I was married that I realized that I did not know how to handle conflict. I was the oldest of four children in my home growing up and most often had the responsibility of taking care of my younger siblings. When it came to disagreements with them, I pretty much had the say-so. I never truly found myself in a situation where I had to compromise and work with someone hand in hand to come to a resolution. Unfortunately, when I saw conflict in my home between my parents, I never actually saw first-hand how they handled their disagreements. There would be an argument one day and the next day, it was as if nothing ever happened. When I got married, I could not figure out how in the world they did that! How could you be so upset with someone one day and then the next day act like all was good. Not seeing my parents work through their problems and 'talk it out', I did not know how to do that for my relationship. It would be years before I learned to truly respect my husband and take control of my own emotions and actions. This was a challenging road to take, especially without godly wisdom and encouragement.

Early on in my relationship, we were not active in church and the faith we have now was non-existent. I was very naive and just honestly did not know what it meant to be a wife, especially not a wife that was pleasing to the Lord. Don't get me wrong, when it comes to submission, I truly believe my mother and grandmother were prime examples of what submission was supposed to look like. I just didn't recognize it until I was older. Gaining knowledge, wisdom, and understanding on how to be a better wife is so vital and is productive. Just like there is no rule book for being a good parent, there is no guideline on how to be a wife. Gleaning knowledge from books, reading materials, and other wives is greatly beneficial to learning how to be the very best wife you can be. Choose to be productive in this area and continuously look for godly material (including your Bible) to be educated. Connecting with other godly women, whether through your local church, social media or family and friends, can give an insight that you may have never thought to consider important for your marriage. There are times when we may not recognize that we may need to work on an area until someone points out that they were dealing with the same thing.

    I recall a time when speaking with a very influential woman of GOD, she shared with me an experience where she had to take up for her husband when someone said something she did not like. I don't remember what was said because I was so admired by the fact that she 'took up for her man'. It sounds simple enough and almost would seem to be a given to take up for the one you love, but I had never been in a situation where I felt I had to do the same. On top of that, I almost always had the impression that James can take care of himself, he doesn't need me to do that. To hear a first-hand account of this opened my eyes to see that standing up for your husband is productive and shows a lot of respect. As a wife, I should be the first one on his side and the first one to speak up for anything and everything that goes against him as a man. Especially when in the presence of someone who is speaking negatively about him.

    Titus 2: 3-5 encourages the older women to teach younger women and help them to be better wives to their husband. There are some wonderful, GOD-fearing women out here that would love to give you some knowledge on how to be successful in your marriage relationship. A lot of which, who may have had to learn what they know the hard way. How awesome it is to get the knowledge now and avoid disaster later! Then, who knows, you might end up on the giving end of the conversation.

It's a matter of life-and-death in a lot of circumstances. If you don't do this now you will die... and soon. A death that is so painful and filled with regret that you wish you could have approached life differently. But it is too late to go back now. You are so far gone, GOD Almighty Himself will not turn back the time. If things don't change right now, in 3 to 6 months at the most, it's all going to end. Sounds pretty serious and intense, doesn't it? You are most likely thinking that I've gone too far and it's not that serious. Life and death situations only happen when someone is committing major sin against GOD. Why would someone die from something as simple as submission? This death I am referring to is so much deeper. This death encompasses not only your physical, but also includes your mental and emotional wellbeing. The lack of submission causes this death, as well as the lack of productivity in submission. Again, you cannot live life being your husband's doormat, or anyone else's for that matter. It's more than just trying to please GOD by not sinning. We must move and do what He says. It's like the story told in Matthew chapter 25. The master gave each of his three servants a certain number of talents. All but one of the servants took the talents and made a profit from what the master gave them. The one who did not, because he chose to hide his talent, got his talent taken away from him! Why? Because The Most High gave all His children gifts and we are to use them for His glory. We belong to Him, He purchased us, redeemed us, and gave us all work to do, and that work is very valuable. It was not to sit idle by hiding from the world, waiting for Christ's return. Marriage is work and it takes productivity to please GOD in it and make a return on the investment.

American Cancer Society's FAQ page describes terminal illness or a terminal condition as an irreversible illness that in the near future will result in death or a state of permanent unconsciousness from which the person is unlikely to recover.

When it comes to diagnosing a person with a terminal condition and giving timeframes on how long a person must live, doctors and professionals go to great extents and do everything they can within their human capabilities. Without knowing for a fact, the lifespan of a terminally ill patient, they often try to give an optimistic amount of time based on the severity of the situation. If the person lives longer than the specified amount of time, that's great but if not, then it becomes heartbreaking and very challenging to settle the minds of grieving friends and families. When all that can be done has been tried, and a person has reached the end, he/she (including family and friends) finds themselves in a place preparing for death. The process takes a physical, emotional, and mental toll on all that are involved.

The lack of submission in a marriage relationship can and will often result in a terminal condition that leads to death or a state of permanent unconsciousness in the grace of life. This death or state of unconsciousness comes first from not obeying GOD Most High. After all, to be successful in submission to your spouse, you must first know how to submit to the authority of GOD Almighty. We have been commanded to love the Lord GOD, walk in His ways, and keep His commands. When we choose to do this, GOD will bless, and His blessing includes life and increase. To follow GOD Almighty and His word is not too hard or too difficult. We must speak life with our mouths and keep His word in our hearts. It is when we turn our hearts away and don't submit that we are destroyed, and our lives shortened. To have a life without submission to GOD Most High is no life at all. It leads to death, eternal.

When it comes to terminally ill marriage relationships, who is to say how long you will survive? No doctor or health care professional can take an optimistic approach to this one. Only GOD Most High knows the day and the hour. Of course, death is imminent for all, but if we can live out our last days in increase and prosperity by simply obeying the Lord GOD, Why would someone choose to go a different way? Why would we want to spend our last days bedridden, in hospice care, on a feeding tube, with an IV, a catheter.... terminally ill, permanently unconscious... from a lack of submission? Why allow our marriages to suffer when one act of submission can bring a life of abundant blessings? We can live our last days filled with real joy, love, rest, and peace.

Chapter 2
What is Submission?

One thing to understand about submission is what it is not. It is not being a doormat, a floor rug, or a wet blanket, not even a punching bag for your spouse. Submission can and does take on multiple meanings, and I am sure certain thoughts come to mind when the word is heard; but true submission starts first from within. Your mindset must be in order and working with complete understanding for true submission to be active and productive. A lot of women think of submission as a form of weakness. That in order to be submissive, they have to be controlled. These women have the mindset "I'm not going to have some man tell me what to do!" "I'm a strong and independent woman, I don't need a man." or "I already got a daddy, I don't need another one." Therefore I say your mindset must be in order and with complete understanding. It's the lack of knowledge that causes us to be destroyed. (Hosea 4.6) When one is quick to assume submitting themselves to another is in some way lessening their character, it allows the enemy to come in and distort and even tear apart great relationships. Only when we get a complete and perfect understanding of submission and all it entails, can we then gain victory over the enemy in this area and truly enjoy GOD-ordained marriages successfully.

Honestly speaking, I never thought of submission as an act of cowardness or something that would require me to be under the complete control of my husband. I never thought of it at all. It was not until someone pointed out how submissive I was to my husband (after about 5 years of marriage) that I did start to wonder what it looked like. At the time, a fellow church member asked me how I was able to be so submissive to my husband and allow him to take the lead in everything. I gave a generic answer, like 'just let him do it', but it was at this moment that I took a step back and truly started to question exactly what submission was and what it should look like in marriage relationships. This is when I initially had the idea to write a book about it. It has taken me 10 years to finally get 'pen to paper' and finish this writing. I think back to my mother, grandmother, and the other women in my family. They were truly the epitome of what submission should reflect. Growing up, I saw these women respect their husbands, take care of their homes, go to work every day and still found time to have fun with each other. Once I got married, I was just merely emulating what had been an environment that thrived on the value of having a relationship. Doing what needed to be done, the best way you know how. My mother, grandmother, and my aunts did not give up on their relationships at the first sign of an argument or disagreement. They stood their ground, fought for what was right, and handled business. I have the utmost respect for each of them because I still don't know how they did it, but they made it look easy. After nearly 20 years of marriage, it took me a long time to figure some things out but by the grace of GOD Almighty, He has given me great wisdom and grace to grow and get better every day.

    Submission is not a form of control. It's not being told you better do what I say or it's over. It's not losing sight of who you are so that someone else can take your light. Submission is choosing to do what is right according to the desires of the One who requires it. That One being The Most High, GOD Almighty, The One and Only True AND Living GOD. (I AM)

    All husbands require, desire, and need respect. Submission to him is (in my opinion) the greatest display of respect a wife can give to her husband. You must respect your man to effectively submit to him. Lack of respect = lack of submission. When I submit, I am non-verbally telling my husband I honor his role as head of the household. I respect his opinions, his values, and his decisions. Even if I don't completely agree with every move he makes, I choose to respect my husband fully to allow him to be what Yahweh created him to be (mistakes and all). With this being stated, it's highly imperative that the man you call husband or husband-to-be shares the same values and beliefs (goals, dreams, religion, etc.) Do two walk together unless they have agreed to do so? (Amos 3.3) If the union is not GOD-ordained, that can cause much more heartache and headache that can possibly be avoided. Heartache and headache happen in every relationship, but it's much easier to handle and ease the pain when I can be assured that my spouse not only has my best interest in mind but will work with me and pray with me to overcome every obstacle we face, together. This practice can be incredibly challenging or even non-existent if the union is not on one accord. Don't be unequally yoked.

Any time I am studying or doing any type of research, I always like to look up the definition of the word. A lot of us as people, use words and phrases because we heard someone else say it and do not really know what they mean or what we are even talking about. We just say it because it sounds good. Let's get the fullness of the word submission by getting a few definitions. When looking at the definition of submission, the first part is a noun being defined as the action or fact of accepting or yielding to a superior force or to the will or authority of another person. The second definition is the action of presenting a proposal, application or other document for consideration or judgment. In its Archaic meaning, it's defined as humility and meekness. The remaining definitions are as follows:

- Law: a proposition or argument presented by a lawyer to a judge or jury.
- The condition of being submissive, humble, or compliant. Compliance, conformity, obedience, subordination

Definition of submit: to stop trying to fight or resist something: to agree to do or accept something you have been opposing or resisting. Transitive verb: 1. To yield to governance or authority; to subject to a condition, treatment, or operation. 2. To present or propose to another for review, consideration, or decision Definition of submissive: READY to conform to the authority or will of others; meekly obedient or passive; inclined or ready to submit or yield to the authority of another, unresistingly or humbly obedient. As you can see, there are many layers to the meaning of submit and submission, yet the context remains the same. Subjecting and yielding ourselves to another for the greater good, selfless relationships, and when it comes to the topic of marriage, for the fulfilment of divine covenant; it is a strength we can tap into when we fully grasp the meaning.

When asking multiple women how they define submission, it is almost always defined as an act that only pertains to marriage. As if submission only applies to women who are married or in a committed relationship with a man. And it's warranted, being that we live in a society that says submission is when a wife lives by what her husband tells her what to do and that's it. NOT TRUE! When we take time to honestly think about our life situations and how we live, we soon realize that we submit to many things every day, all the time. The parent who submits to the care of her adult children, even against better judgement, every employee that has an employer, and ultimately any relationship where all parties involved understand the importance of give and take.

Submission is the continual action of love being shown physically, mentally, emotionally, and spiritually. It encompasses every fabric of your being. It is choosing to fulfill the very best of who you are in each of these areas, with the understanding that you are only as whole as your willingness to submit to transformation, progress, and change. Submission is allowing The Most High to be number One in your life, knowing that His way is always better, bigger and more effective. It is choosing to fulfill His promises and purpose for your life while walking in the Fruit of the Spirit to give your spouse the opportunity to do the same. In this continual process, we will experience growth.

As we grow older, change is bound to happen. I know after 20 years of marriage I am not the same 19-year-old that was standing before the preacher man when I said, "till death do we part." I will admit I did not know what that fully meant until I went through some things. We have had some good times and we have had some really bad times, but submission was the key to my stance to be with my husband through whatever. It is the change that is inevitable that puts the pressure on our choice to submit. We can choose to work to have a successful marriage, an unproductive marriage, or no marriage at all. Whatever the choice, it takes work, and it takes submission.

Submission is obedience. Obedience to The Most High is of the utmost importance. Obedience and submission go hand-in-hand. To be truly submissive, obedience must be first and foremost.

Those that are the sons and daughters of GOD Most High are led by His Spirit. (Romans 8.14) To allow yourself to be led, you must submit to His Spirit. In that submission, I can receive instruction from GOD Himself. When I obey that instruction, it's the greatest act of love I can show to the Father. That obedience creates trust. And trust brings intimacy in relationships. GOD will show Himself so mighty because He can now trust me with everything. Through my acts of obedience, I've proven my love, devotion, and ultimately, my submission to Him. Submission is so important and very necessary in everyday life. Ultimately, it is a requirement if we want to fulfill the plan of GOD in our lives. There are many examples in the Word that show us how important it is to be obedient to GOD Almighty and to be submitted to His plan. I am reminded of King Saul in the Old

Testament Scriptures. In 1 Samuel chapter 13, King Saul was gathered with the people of Israel and were preparing for another battle. He was commanded to go to Gilgal and wait seven days for the Prophet Samuel to come and offer a burnt sacrifice to the Lord. King Saul went as told, and waited the seven days, however when he saw that Samuel did not come right away, he decided to offer the sacrifice himself. He basically became impatient and allowed the actions of the people around him to respond in a way that was disobedient to GOD. Samuel showed up as soon as he was done with the offering! King Saul had done a "foolish thing" and had not kept the "command the Lord GOD gave" him. GOD Almighty rejected King Saul and literally stripped his kingdom away from him because of his disobedience! No second chances and no opportunity to get it right. When you read the text, you see that it wasn't the fact he gave an offering that was wrong because other kings after him had done the same (by command of the Lord), but it was because he disobeyed a direct command given from God to the Prophet Samuel. He was told that his kingdom would not continue because of his act of disobedience. King Saul decided in a moment of desperation to take matters into his own hands, and it turned against him.

  This example may seem extreme to some, but it's just like us in many of our own personal life situations. We know what needs to be done, GOD Almighty has given us the direction, and has even sent a trusted friend to confirm the truth for us, but at the first sign of trouble, we get nervous. In that moment of anxiousness, we step out before time and mess up the entire plan of GOD. Now we are scrambling and are all over the place trying to figure out how to get ourselves out of the mess. Thanks be to Lord Jesus, we now have mercy and grace through Him, and we can ask for forgiveness and get another chance to try again. It all comes down to choice. Just like in marriage, we can choose to have a successful one and work at it, we can choose to submit to GOD Almighty and follow His lead in our everyday life circumstances.

Choose submission to keep the order and balance. GOD Almighty does all things in order and His plans are always done according to His will for our lives. When we choose to go our own way and make our own plans, the results are often unfavorable. We find ourselves in positions that we cannot get ourselves out of. Psalms 37.5 says "Commit thy way unto the LORD; trust also in Him; and He shall bring it to pass." Commitment requires one to confidently entrust themselves. In doing this unto the LORD, submission is key to doing it successfully. We must literally roll our life journey on to GOD Most High and allow Him to take the lead and the reigns, no matter how difficult our circumstances or situations. After we give it to Him, we must fully lean on Him, completely rely on Him, and have confidence in Him.

Submission demands a priority check. When submitting to GOD Most High is our primary focus, our priorities will automatically fall right in order. For all of us, that should be GOD Almighty first, family second, then ministry, employment, and everything else would follow in line in its respective places according to your needs and wants. Any additional assignments, plans or goals will fall in place and order as what is necessary and important for you and your life journey. Matthew 22.37 tells us that we must love the Lord our GOD with all our hearts, and souls and our minds, going on to say in verse thirty-eight that this is the first and greatest command. When we truly take into consideration what Jesus Christ is saying in this verse, we all must admit, we fall short in this area. Very few of us actually love GOD this much and in this way. To love Him with everything means He is all I think about, dream about, talk about, imagine, plan for, plan with, live for, etc. How many of us can honestly say that GOD Most High is EVERYTHING? All the time? If this is you sister, hey I commend you, sincerely, and I am truly proud of you. For the rest of us... Life is real. Life is hard and sometimes it sucks. Just because life sucks, I don't allow any of that to take away from the sovereignty of The Most High. My sucky moments in life do not make my Lord and Savior any less powerful in any way at all. It is in those less than favorable moments, that I desire and push myself to lean to Him the most. I may not be in a position to talk about GOD Most High in every waking moment, but I can most certainly try to invite him into the conversation. In the challenging moments, is when my submission to GOD Almighty highlights His priority in my life. When things get hard, do I submit to His Will and declare His promises for my life or do I cower to my disbeliefs and doubts with no expectation for change? The Lord may not be the first thought, but He tops the list, and that is a start! And let's face it, we all have to start somewhere! When we choose to be submissive in our relationships, first to our Heavenly Father, then to our husbands, we will purposefully keep our priorities in order to ensure our every action pleases the Lord and that we respect our spouses. Make a valid effort to keep the priorities in order and eventually you will find that GOD does make it FIRST in your list! When submission is important to us, I believe we can fulfill the Scripture verses Matthew 22.37-38 that tell us to love GOD with our all and to love our neighbor as ourselves.

Your husband is your neighbor! Any time the topic of love is brought up in a sermon or biblical teaching, this passage of Scripture is going to be included. I often ponder the question, how can we truly love our neighbor as ourselves, if we don't love ourselves first? A lot of us don't love us. We get up every day and go through the motions, wishing we were thinner, bigger, smarter, smaller, more of this and less of that. Never truly satisfied with what we have, who we are, and how we look. So, if we expect to love our husbands unconditionally while submitting to them and respecting them, we are going to have to work on loving ourselves as well. Love is an action that has to be evident and sincere for submission to be productive in our marriage relationships. When looking at the translation of love in that particular verse, we find that it means to love *by embracing GOD's will, choosing to do His choices and obeying them through His power*. It also translates as *'to prefer to love, to long for, to take pleasure in.'* It literally tells us that this type of love is a choice, but also that it is only effective through obedience and by the power of the Holy Ghost. Lord knows, it is only by His Spirit that I can genuinely love James and submit to that man!

    Take time to reflect on where you are in your spiritual and mental well-being right now. Get out pen and paper and take inventory on everything that is going on in your life that could be or is a hindrance to you truly loving yourself. Be honest with yourself and take genuine steps to make progressive change in those areas. As you work on loving yourself, you will find it much easier to love your husband. My attitude towards myself always reflected on how I treated my husband. Every time I felt as though I was unattractive and not sexy, it would affect our intimacy in the bedroom. I honestly would not wear the sexy night gown or any lingerie at all. Oversized t-shirts, comfy pajama pants, and thick socks every night! I can recall numerous times when James would tell me how beautiful I was and, in my head, I am shooting down every compliment with a negative thought. "Yeah right, I am so fat! How could you think I am beautiful?" "I don't know what he sees, because all I see is flab!" "I've gained so much weight it's ridiculous!" The thoughts would go on and on. For every compliment, I had a counterattack. It was if I had a loaded weapon and emptied the clip every chance I got. This was a destructive behavior pattern for me, and it was not pleasing to the Lord. I was failing to submit my thoughts to Him and think of things that were true, pure, and lovely. (Philippians 4.8)

When we consider our husbands as our neighbor, our perspectives and how we treat them would certainly change. For some of us, when we see our neighbor, we are very cordial. We smile and wave and say hello, asking them how they are doing. They see us looking well and even if we don't feel like talking or being nice, we do it anyway. There is even the nosy neighbor who is in everybody's business, that you will tolerate. I do realize this is not everyone and not every neighbor. I know of some people that never talk to their neighbors. They don't know their names, they don't even wave hello. Sounds like some marriages as well. You live in the same place and see each other every day but never say good morning and having conversations is non-existent. In the case of cordial neighbors, if some spouses treated their husbands like the next-door neighbor, there would be change. Having the 'my husband is my neighbor perspective' would cause you to ask your spouse "Hey, how are you today?" every time you saw him. No matter how you were feeling or what you were going through, you would put on a smile and say, "It's good to see you; hope you enjoy your day!" "This weather is awesome today!" "Tell the family I said hello!" You would choose to have a conversation. You would choose to smile and shake hands. You would take time out of your day to spend a few minutes with someone else. You make the choice to put aside how you feel to give time to someone else. The point is, oftentimes we treat complete strangers better than our own spouses. We will show respect and reverence to people we don't even know (all day long) but when it comes to our husbands, we'll give them the worst part of us, as if they don't deserve to be treated just as worthy. Why is that? How can we go to work speaking proper and polite to our co-workers, employers, employees, then go home and speak to the husband as if he offended you just by looking at you? Somewhere along the way, respect was lost. Somewhere along the way, submission was not an active part of the relationship. Somewhere along the way, you failed to keep The Most High first.

As I have mentioned before and will continue to reiterate throughout this book, we must keep priorities in order and in check. GOD Almighty must be first. There must be an understanding of what submission is and what it looks like. We need to be submitted to GOD Almighty first and foremost, then we will be better equipped to submit to our husbands (as they submit to GOD Almighty) and respect them in their roles as head of the household. This is so important to ensure the quality of our marriages stay fulfilling and in the will of GOD. When we do this and actively work to keep this order in our lifestyles, we can recognize the enemy when he tries to come in and disrupt things in our marriages.

Submission is important and necessary because the Bible commands it. More than once. And not just submit to HIM. Ephesians 5.20 - 21 says to "Give thanks always for all things unto God and the Father in the name of our Lord Jesus Christ; submitting yourselves one to another in the fear of God." (KJV). There are other versions that read be 'subject' to one another. Submit and subject are one in the same. We submit to one another out of reverence to the Lord Jesus Christ and out of fear. Not because we are looking to control each other or even to put ourselves in a place of power (although, there are those that do just that, unfortunately), but because we genuinely care for others and their well-being. As Believers, we should always walk in the place of love, looking to serve others in every way possible. If this is our thought process and even more, how we think we should be, how much more should we be this way with our own spouses.

There are countless Sundays and Wednesdays where believers go to their church homes and serve. We sing in the choir, volunteer for the usher board, help cook meals on Family and Friends Day, some even watch the children in the daycare.

We look for countless ways to serve in the church, doing our due diligence, submitting ourselves to others and GOD through the ministries of the church. All so that we can feel like we are serving our purpose and doing our part. However, when it comes to our husbands, we look for plenty of excuses to not engage, participate, and be of service. We are too tired, too busy, or we have a headache! We give and we give, whether to gain the accolades, the attention, the praise or the satisfaction that comes with it, however, that same energy becomes void when it comes to our marriages. Believe it or not, but men want some attention too! They want to be loved. They want to know that you see them and acknowledge their efforts. If it is being a provider, going to work every day, taking care of some chores around the home, paying the bills, putting gas in the car, changing the baby's diaper, cooking dinner, regardless if it's large or small, they want you to appreciate them. Something as simple as "thank you for taking care of dinner today" or "I appreciate you for making sure the bills are paid" can go a long way for your husband's emotional well-being.

Showing appreciation in this way may be hard for some of you wives that may be reading this. I know because I was in a position for a very long time where I was the wife that went to work every day and still had to come home and cook, clean, and do laundry every day. All while my husband came and went as he pleased. Thank the Lord we did not have any children at this time of our relationship because I don't know how I would have reacted if we did. Telling him 'Thank you' for anything was the farthest thing from my mind. With everything I was doing, he needed to be thanking me! Even in this season of life when I felt as though I was doing everything, I had to find the good in my situation. Yes, I was working every single day, coming home having to cook dinner, wash dishes, clean the bathroom, vacuum the floors, make the bed, and do the laundry, it wasn't all bad. My husband made sure all the bills were paid, he drove me to work every day, making sure I was on time, picked me up on time, ensured I had everything I needed and wanted, and often bought me gifts just because. We as wives must find the energy to show appreciation and love for our husbands. We can no longer give all of ourselves to everyone and everything and then give our husbands the leftovers, expecting them to understand. We can no longer have the mindset that it is okay to treat everyone outside of our home with honor and respect and those within it with our negative outpours because they should understand. We must make the choice today to stand in the truth of GOD's word. As hard as it may seem, take the time to find the good in your husband. Remember why you married him and write it down. Write down all the reasons why he deserves respect and why you should submit to him as his wife. You may not feel it right now, but trust me, do it anyway and you will look back on this moment and realize it was all a part of the plan.

We were born to be submissive! The society we live in and the culture we have grown accustomed to, would demand that submission is a form of control that women should no longer be required to uphold. However, submission is necessary to be successful in this society. Living in a time where so many decide to be 'life partners', rather than married, and so many homosexual couples have been accepted as the normal family, it can be very distracting to focus on what is right and important in GOD Almighty's eyes.

From the time you came out of your mother's womb, you were in a place of submission. Our entire childhood life required an act of submission and obedience to our parents, elders, and authority figures in our lives. We were taught to respect our elders, listen to authorities, obey the laws set in place, and be a friend to those in need. Everything we encounter in life revolves around submission.

In the courtroom, the defendant is subject to the lawyer, who is subject to the Judge and the marshals (1 Peter 2.13-14).

In your home, your children are subject to your rules. You are subject to your utility providers, because if you don't pay your bills, you're subject to disconnection or interruption of service. The student is subject to the teacher who in turn is subject to the principal, who also answers to a superior. I am sure by now you see the point I am making when it comes to submission and subjection in our everyday lives; and maybe you have thought of some other scenarios where this case is true. With that, I pray you have come to agree with me that we are wired to be submissive.

Every authority ever created comes from GOD Almighty. He is our Creator, and we are commanded to submit to Him. Submit yourselves therefore to God. James 4.7a. GOD Almighty is the highest Authority, and every living thing is submitted to Him.

Our greatest example of submission was Jesus Christ Himself. While here on Earth, He showed us exactly what that looks like. Jesus will always be our greatest example and teacher of submission. He, with all power in His hands, understood His role while on Earth and not once did He put Himself before or above His Heavenly Father and do His own thing. Everything He did was because of direct instruction from the Father. He recognized GOD Almighty's authority and submitted. When we do as Jesus did and follow His commandments, we stand firm upon the Rock and cannot be shaken. (Luke 6.48). Jesus said if we love Him, we will do what He says (John 14.15). Doing what the Lord says over our own agenda will require the utmost denial of self and obedience to Him.

Jesus got full on submission! He said His meat is to do the will of Him (Father GOD Almighty) that sent Him, and to finish His work (John 4.34). Jesus Christ lived a life of submission. He even prayed submissively. Jesus Christ understood that His prayer life was His lifeline and His only way of communication with the Father while on Earth. Because the earthly task was so great, He ensured that His prayers were not only the center of His life, but also lined up with the Will of the Father. Our prayers must be the same way if we expect to see the greatness and promises The Most High has in store for us. Praying the Will of GOD takes submitting to the Will of GOD, humbly and respectfully. If we consider GOD Almighty as our Heavenly Father, why would we not submit to His authority as such? The Lord Jesus showed us in the truest form what that looks like. Father, I pray now in the name of Jesus Christ that each one of us chooses to submit to You, Your Will, and Your Way for our lives. We want to make you first place in everything and do what You say at all times. We trust that as we humbly submit to You, You will give us every promise mentioned in Your Word for those who submit to You in godly reverence. We believe by faith that You hear us and will answer as we call out to You. Amen.

Allow the presence of GOD to encamp your entire being and trust the process. Submission may not be your first resort when it comes to difficult situations in your life, but I believe as you strive to be more submissive to GOD, it will be easier to submit in your marriage relationship.

Chapter 3
Real Joy

I've heard it said many times that joy is not the same as happiness. That to have real joy is a state of being that is only experienced spiritually. Real joy comes from within. I must agree with this statement. Happiness is truly an emotion that comes and goes, but joy is deep within your soul and is always there, whether you are happy or sad. The Scripture says in Nehemiah 8.10 "The joy of the Lord is your strength and your stronghold." Interestingly, these words were said during a service where the people of GOD were brought to tears after hearing the laws of GOD! How many times has that happened to us? We read the Bible and think to ourselves, how in the world am I supposed to live my life in this way and please GOD? It's enough to make you cry! Thanks be to Jesus, we can, and it is possible. Just like Ezra encouraged the people to eat and drink and not worry in this 8th chapter of Nehemiah, we must encourage ourselves with the promises of His Holy Word, "the joy of the Lord is MY strength!" Even when life gets hard and struggles get in the way, we still can find a reason to have joy.

In the book of Galatians Chapter 5 verse 22 it says, "The Fruit of the Spirit is love, joy, peace, patience, kindness, goodness, faithfulness, gentleness, and self-control." This Fruit is the very character of God Most High. Character traits do not come and go, they exhibit themselves as who we are even when no one is looking. When we are born again Believers of Jesus Christ, joy is a promised trait that we possess as the Holy Spirit fills us. We must submit to His calling and tap into that which has been given. When we receive the Holy Spirit and truly line our spirits with Him, we experience that real unspeakable joy.

That joy that is unexplainable, yet completely satisfying. The joy that makes you wonder, how in GOD's green earth are you able to still have peace in such chaos. Real joy. It's not superficial and it's not moveable like the wind. It comes with complete submission to the Lord.

Nevertheless, just like with any fruit, growth comes with time. A farmer does not plant apple seeds one day then get apples next week. There is a process that must take place when it comes to experiencing the joys in this life, especially when so many of us are used to burying ourselves in drama, stress, worry, fears, and the cares of the world. Yes, the Fruit of the Spirit is ours and should be evident in our lives once we have accepted Christ, however if you struggled with patience before salvation and were doing nothing to practice being better at it, that same struggle will be there after salvation. The advantage you have now that you are saved, is that you have the Lord Jesus Christ and His Holy Spirit to help grow in patience for that Fruit to become evident and not only evident but also to remain. The LORD Jesus Christ has chosen you, and in choosing you, He also appointed you so that as you should go out and produce fruit, fruit that remains, so that whatever you ask the Father, in His name, it will be given to you! (John 15.16)

All too often we as people fool ourselves into thinking we should have certain things in life - certain advantages, perks, and favors -and yet we are not doing anything especially important or favorable to get those advantages. We have the mindset that GOD owes us a good life because we have been doing so good when truthfully our good works have been done from a heart of selfish ambition. The mindset is not one of servanthood, but rather what am I going to get in return for all this work? Too many have the thought process, 'I do this and that, they should at least do this for me!' So, we treat GOD the same way. 'I prayed today Father. I read my Word every day for two weeks. You should bless me because that's a record for me!' What happened to doing things out of love? I thought the joy of the Lord was your strength. When the joy of the Lord is your strength, you read, pray, and worship not out of obligation or to get a reward, but because those things truly STRENGTHEN YOU and that brings you REAL JOY. You do not need any attention or accolades from people. The work you choose to do to help others comes from a place of humility and servitude and not want and obligation. Whatever you do, do it enthusiastically, as something done for the LORD and not for men, knowing that you will receive the reward of an inheritance from the LORD. We serve the LORD Christ. (Colossians 3.23-24)

When we find this real joy in the Lord, we will find it in our marriages. The intimacy in our marriage relationships brings real joy and sets us apart from other marriages. We have all seen couples where you can tell that something is different about them. Where they just seem to be genuinely "happy". As if they possess something that everyone else is missing. I truly believe that submission is that "something" missing. It comes down to this. For a fruit tree to grow and bear fruit, it must first take root in a properly cultivated ground. Its roots must run deep into the dark, moist, nutrient dense environment to grow thick and strong enough taking in the proper elements to carry throughout the rest of the plant. The roots and plant system must be grown and well established for years before the fruit even starts to bloom. All the while it withstands the seasons of nature that constantly change around it -summer, winter, spring, and fall. Rainy days and the scorching sun. Through it all it never stops growing and if it is well tended, it will continually bear fruit year after year. It submits to its environment to grow the way it was designed. When we properly cultivate our marriages, submitting ourselves to GOD's design and then to each other, we will grow. No matter the situations or circumstances that may arise in our relationships, we will thrive. Our atmosphere, our conditions will always remain conducive for us to bear nutritious fruit in season. Challenges are going to come; we are often going to be faced with decisions that will require a godly response. Real joy that exudes from the inside will display godly responses outwardly.

So here is the formula: (Ephesians 5)

- Husband and Wife submit to The Most High
- Husband submits to The Most High, to his wife and loves her and presents her.
- Wife submits to The Most High, submits to her husband, and respects him.
- Husband and Wife experience favor, grace, the abundant life, and all that comes with it:

The Love of their Heavenly Father, the Covering and Friendship of the Lord and Savior Jesus Christ, the Comfort and Leading of the Holy Spirit and the Fruit of His Spirit AND EVERY PROMISE written in the Bible! It is amazing to me. The couple that emulates this cannot help but look different! We all can and should all have this!

The saying, 'the world didn't give me joy and the world can't take it away'. So, what exactly is joy? Most individuals, spiritual or otherwise, conclude that joy is a feeling deep on the inside of which does not change because of situations or circumstances. It's not an emotion fueled by external happenings. But it is a feeling of spiritual contentment that resonates, 'I am happy and delighted and no matter what comes my way, I am good with life.'

Dictionary.com defines joy as the emotion of great delight or happiness caused by something exceptionally good or satisfying. I like the 'Christian joy' explained by John Piper (desiringGod.org), which states, "joy is a good feeling in the soul, produced by the Holy Spirit, as He causes us to see the beauty of Christ in the Word and in the world". I personally view it as a as head of the house]. Husband, love your wives [seek the highest good for her and surround her with a caring, unselfish love], just as Christ also loved the church and gave Himself up for her, so that he might sanctify the church, having cleansed her by the washing of water with the word [of GOD], so that [in turn] He might present the church to Himself in glorious splendor, without spot or wrinkle or any such thing; but that she would be holy [set apart for GOD] and blameless. Even so husbands should and are morally obligated to love their own wives as [being in a sense] their own bodies. He who loves his own wife loves himself. For no one ever hated his own body, but [instead] he nourishes and protects and cherishes it, just as Christ does the church, because we are members (parts) of His body. FOR THIS REASON, A MAN SHALL LEAVE HIS FATHER AND HIS MOTHER AND SHALL BE JOINED [and be faithfully devoted] TO HIS WIFE, AND THE TWO SHALL BECOME ONE FLESH. This mystery [of two becoming one] is great; but I am speaking with reference to [the relationship of] Christ and the church. However, each man among you [without exception] is to love his wife as his very own self [with behavior worthy of respect and esteem, always seeking the best for her with an attitude of lovingkindness], and the wife [must see to it] that she respects and delights in her husband [that she notices him and prefers him and treats him with loving concern, treasuring him, honoring him, and holding him dear]." AMP

    Wives are told to submit to their husbands in everything as to the Lord because he is the head, just as Christ is the head of the Church; and, to respect them. Marriage is ordained by GOD Almighty Himself and he reminds us in this passage of Scripture the positions of husband and wife -man and woman are to leave their parents and be joined together as one.

    Colossians 3.18: "Wives, be subject to your husbands [out of respect for their position as protector, and their accountability to God], as is proper and fitting in the LORD." AMP

    This Scripture breaks down the reason for submitting and respecting our husbands and shows that our husbands must take their positions as GOD commands for the marriage to be effective. We as wives have our responsibility to submit and be respectful and must do so regardless of our husband's actions. This can be a challenge when the husband does not want to do what it takes to have a successful marriage. Your prayer life is going to be the foundation to see change in this area. Therefore it is also important to ensure that you are evenly yoked. Meaning you are with the one man GOD desires for you to be with forever. Too many relationships have been joined in holy matrimony till death and there was nothing holy about the union. Seek The Most High first before marriage to know for certain the man you are going to spend the rest of your life with is supposed to be your husband. If you are in a situation where you are already married, I believe The Most High is well able and more than willing to fix our mistakes and help us to make it out of situations where the burden is heavier than the Lord's. Seek wise counsel and pray, pray, pray, pray.

    Proverbs 18.22: "He who finds a [true and faithful] wife finds a good thing and obtains favor and approval from the LORD." AMP

    Yes wife, you are a GOOD thing and because your husband has found you, he is given favor from our Heavenly Father. When your husband is favored, you reap the benefits as well. Why would you not want to submit to a man who is favored by the One and Only True and Living GOD?

    Proverbs 14.1 "The wise woman builds her house [on a foundation of godly precepts, and her household thrives], But the foolish one [who lacks spiritual insight tears it down with her own hands [by ignoring godly principles]." AMP

Submission is a godly principle we as children of GOD should all desire to have. Submission says I choose to do what the LORD says and live my life according to His word. A life submitted to The Most High is a life full of favor and blessings in every area.

Proverbs 19.4 "House and wealth are the inheritance from fathers, but a wise, understanding, and sensible wife is a gift and blessing from the LORD."

You can have all the money in the world, but it will not be enjoyed if you are not happy. Make the decision to live life to the fullest by acting like the gift and blessing that you are. So many unmarried women pray and fast just to have a husband and have yet to experience it. Recognize what a blessing marriage is, what it should look like, and step into your position.

Titus 2.3-5 Speaks to older and young women to have humble behavior, not be gossipers, not be addicted to wine, to love their husband and children, to be submitted to their own husbands, honoring God through His word. God honors submission and we should as well.

As mentioned before, these are just a few verses that touch on being a wife and on marriage. I strongly encourage you to take time to search out the Scriptures for yourself to find help and encouragement. As you dive deep into the Word, I pray that you find the presence of the Almighty comforting your hurt places and fulfilling every empty space with His love and His peace. The Word of God is alive and immensely powerful. Have faith as you read it and you will experience the miraculous. I believe it for you and your marriage.

Chapter 4
I am a Proverbs 31 Woman

I read an article years ago that said no woman can truly fulfill and be the woman described in Proverbs 31.10-31. It stated that the standard penned in the Word is so high, it is unattainable and not meant to be taken literally. I beg to differ! I honestly believe EVERY woman is capable and has the potential to be this woman in all its entirety. This is not to say that every woman should be a homemaker, sewing every single outfit she and her family wears, never sleeping because she is always on '10' taking care of everyone but herself and volunteering at every church function. The virtuous woman is one that is strong and confident in all moral and mental qualities. She is invaluable, trustworthy, thrifty, dutiful, versatile, watchful, joyful, loving, generous and fearless. A Proverbs 31 woman is confident, as she is wise; her family honors her, as well as her community. These are all qualities that every woman can exhibit and maintain daily. It is not impossible or unattainable. Of course, being this woman is going to take work, as does anything of purpose. We don't become these women by sitting idly by watching television, eating snacks all day, waiting for the next best thing to fall into our laps. Will it take sacrifice? YES! Will it take dedication and commitment? Of course! It will take all of this, along with consistency, sincerity, and you guessed it, SUBMISSION. I also strongly believe this can only be accomplished (in its fullness) through the Holy Spirit. We cannot be the Proverbs 31 woman in our own strength. Fulfilling these qualities in our own power is a recipe for disaster. It is only by the power of Holy Spirit, and the strength of the Lord Jesus Christ that we can be the capable wives our husbands need, and others admire. We must look to state of being that comes from purposeful living; making conscious decisions to be joyful and to choose joy over other emotions. It's a fulfilment that brings wholeness to empty places and light to dark situations. For instance, if someone close to me passes away (death), the automatic feeling of sadness, grief, and possibly depression occurs. It's a natural feeling and emotion and it is not wrong to feel this way. Now through my grieving, I choose to make the conscious decision and a purposeful effort to find joy in the situation. That may come from knowing my loved one is no longer hurting, sick, suffering and is now with our Lord. Or with the peace in knowing that my loved one no longer has to be concerned with the dark ways of this world and is now truly free from worry, doubt, and shame. I may have to find comfort in knowing that even though their life may have been cut short, they will not have to deal with the sufferings of this life and all that comes with it. Or knowing that she or he lived well and accomplished all that GOD Most High intended for their life and left a legacy and an inheritance for those of us still here. Whatever I must do to find joy in the situation, I will do it, because I know deep down that, in the situation of death (natural death), it is something promised to everyone. Finding joy in every situation is necessary to cope with life. Finding real joy is only possible in a life that is committed and submitted to a servitude to The Most High.

There have been plenty of occasions in my marriage where I had to rely on the joy of the Lord to get me through. We go through so many ups and downs in our lives, relying solely on emotions will quickly bring you down and cause you to be worn out. Early on in my marriage relationship, I cannot say with full assurance that I knew what marriage was all about and I did not know what it meant to be a wife. I feel I saw submissiveness firsthand through the relationships of my parents and grandparents, but never really had an upbringing or teaching to tell me how to be an effective wife. My mother was and still is a very humble woman. Absolutely beautiful inside and out. And I am not saying that just because she is my mother. She genuinely is one of the most wonderful women I know. So, when it comes to submissiveness, my Momma had like it was second nature. Growing up I never once saw her go against the authority or word of my dad. She was always on his side, even if she knew he was wrong. If there ever was an argument, she spoke her mind, stood her ground, even if she disagreed, but never once did I ever see her not stay by my father's side. She always respected him regardless of the situation. How she did that I do not know. How she was able to have an argument with my dad one day and then be cordial and friends like nothing ever happened the next day absolutely baffled me. I mean if I got mad or upset with little brother or sister, I'm not walking around all honkey dory like nothing ever happened afterward. That anger is going to sit around and fester a little bit. At least for a few days. I mean, what the heck, my feelings were hurt! As long as I am upset, I am not talking. I would literally keep quiet and if I did speak, it would be short, one-word responses to questions someone else asked. I am grateful to have seen firsthand the submissiveness of my Momma as a wife, however what I did not see was conflict resolution.

  Conflict resolution was a tough pill to swallow in my marriage. As I said, when I got upset, I was really, really upset and had no problem holding a grudge and playing the quiet game until I felt like my husband understood the severity of my hurt. My anger would stew for days, and the silent game would fuel the pot. While the silent treatment may have worked when I was child, in my marriage it was a different story. I would get upset with James, which happened often, and instead of understanding and compromising with my vow to not talk until he apologized and saw the error of his ways, he gave me the exact same response. Silence. "Okay, now which part of this silent treatment did you not understand?" "I don't talk and don't expect me to talk until you (James) apologize for making me upset!" Uh, yeah did not happen. James was just as stubborn as I was and had no problem waiting until I got out of my feelings and opened my mouth to speak. It would take years for me to open and voice my issues rather than hold them in, waiting on apologies that really did not need to happen.

How did I find joy in this? When conflict is an area that is a part of life and something we will all deal with in our marriages, we need to have a good plan of resolution before they arise. I really wish I had some guidance in this area before and during my marriage relationship. It would have saved me years of heartache and depression. Although, I am still grateful because now I can say what I went through has made me a stronger woman and better equipped to help other women who may be going through the same thing. I think this is a good time to be reminded of our Scripture which comes from 1 Peter 3:1-2. The Christian Standard Bible reads "In the same way, wives, submit yourselves to your own husbands so that, even if some disobey the word, they may be won over without a word by the way their wives live when they observe your pure, reverent lives. Oftentimes when conflict comes, we as women, quickly look for reasons to be right. We must justify why we did what we did and the reason why we did it. Even if we are wrong. Or maybe you are the one who cowers when conflict comes. Instead of facing the situation and dealing with problems, you run from them. A conflict arises and you just keep living life like nothing has happened.

The word joy and variations of it appear over 200 times in the King James Version of the Bible. It must be important to The Most High to mention it that many times! To learn that joy is mentioned this many times gives me hope in knowing I can go to the Scriptures during any season of life for encouragement and have that joy manifested in my situation.

Being truly submissive in marriage brings on this real joy. This real joy is not because you have the best spouse in the world. It's not because you communicate well or not at all, it's not because of great sex or the lack thereof. Submission is the key! Being a wife is a job and there are guidelines and rules, policies and procedures that must be followed and adhered to for success and promotion. I can almost hear someone saying, "What are you talking about?" How can there be guidelines and rules to being a wife? There is no manual that tells me how I am supposed to handle the role of wife in my marriage. If you have made it to this chapter, then you know exactly what I am about to say next. Yes, you guessed it, the Bible is our manual and guideline on how to be godly wives. The Word of God Almighty tells us exactly what we need to be and how to conduct ourselves, as women, as wives, as His children. When we choose to become children of God Almighty in humble obedience, it requires making Jesus Christ LORD over your life. For Him to be LORD, we must be in position to give Him control over every area of our lives, allowing Him to tell us what to do. Submission flows in that vein. The Bible tells us what to do to be successful in our marriages, we need only submit, follow, and obey the rules, policies, and procedures. There are many Scriptures that tell us how we should be as wives and what wives should not be. There are also verses that we can look at that do not point to wives specifically, however, can be applied as such because we are His children. Below are just a few verses for you to reference; please take time to look these verses up, read and study them.

Ephesians 5.22-33 "Wives, be subject to your own husbands, as [a service] to the Lord. For the husband is head of the wife, as Christ is head of the church, Himself being the Savior of the body. But as the church is subject to Christ, so also wives should be subject to their husbands in everything [respecting both their position as protector and their responsibility to GOD

GOD Most High and His Will for our lives to be successful. Being a Proverbs 31 woman is His Will. Why would GOD have this woman in His Word if it were not possible to be this woman? It is because we can be her and spiritually, we are, in all of its entirety. Declare the following verses out loud daily and with confidence that you are this woman. Every time you may feel incapable of being her, declare the Word over yourself. Every time you may feel inadequate, or that you may be falling short in an area, declare the Word out loud. Through good and bad, trials and hardships, happiness, and pain, we can do all things through Christ Who strengthens us. Find joy in the Lord because He is your strength. So, a woman thinks, so is she! And she thinks very highly of herself in the eyes of GOD Almighty. You are the apple of His eye! Whether you are the stay-at-home mommy constantly on the go with you little ones or the mom who works full time outside of the home; you are valuable and you are necessary. With the never-ending laundry, full sink of dishes, picking up toys for the tenth time today; you are capable and full of the Holy Spirit to do and be the woman GOD has called you to be. This is not the time to compare yourself to the next woman who seems to have it all together. I assure you that woman is dealing with similar issues and struggles. We are all striving to be better and wanting to become more. Even if you are the woman who does not have any children or your children are grown, your submission to GOD rests in obedience to His Word. We must find ourselves spiritually secure in our identity that is found in His presence.

  It wasn't until I looked to GOD and not others that I was able to recognize my true potential. I was always told growing up that I could be whatever I wanted to be -a doctor, a lawyer, a police officer. The same thing all well-meaning parents tell their children. As I have grown, I have learned that this statement is not true. I could not be whatever I wanted to be, not really, no matter how hard I tried. What I could be and what I am constantly becoming, is the woman that GOD wants me to be. I strived for many years wanting to please and get the approval of others -my parents, my teachers, my husband. I worked very hard to hear these people tell me I did a good job. That my works were to be noticed and worthy to be praised. In my efforts to appease others, I lost sight of who I was and even more what I was truly destined to do in this life. I honestly felt like if I did not do my best in whatever I put myself to, my parents or my husband would not be pleased with me. I needed to do a good job to be accepted. As a child, that was making good grades and making sure my chores exceeded expectations. As a wife, that was doing whatever my husband asked of me even if it was wrong or made me feel bad. I had no voice and no one to call me out to tell me I had one. It would be years before I learned my identity could only be found in Christ, and He would show me who I was supposed to be in life. My purpose, my destiny, my calling, and my voice would be called out by The GOD of the universe, and He showed me, me. I was lost and He found me. Actually, He found me, and by the power of His Holy Spirit and the work of the Cross of Jesus Christ, I now know who I am. I need only focus on pleasing Him, and the good works that I do now will bring glory to Him.

The same is true for you woman of GOD. Look to Him for guidance, seek Him to find your voice, your place, your standard, your identity and you will be EVERYTHING The Most High GOD has called you to be.

  The following verses have been arranged so they can be declared in a personal way. Recite it often, daily if necessary. Read the verses out loud and believe by faith that you are this woman and/or striving to be her. Even if you may not be fulfilling every Scripture in your life right now, know that it is possible because you can do all things through Christ. He is who strengthens you and He will encourage you if you let Him. Allow the Holy Spirit to lead you in all your endeavors.

The context of the scriptures has not been changed. (Adapted from the Amplified Version of the Bible)

I am an excellent woman, one who is spiritual, capable, intelligent, and virtuous. My value is more precious than jewels and my worth is far above rubies or pearls. The heart of my husband trusts in me with secure confidence, and he will have no lack of gain. I comfort, encourage and am only good to him and not evil all the days of my life. I look for wool and flax and work with willing hands in delight. I am like the merchant ships, abounding with treasure; I bring food for my household from far away. I also rise while it is still night and give food to my household and assign tasks to my maids. I consider a field before I buy or accept, expanding my business prudently. With my profits I plant fruitful vines in my vineyard. I equip myself with strength- spiritual, mental, and physical fitness for my God-given task, making my arms strong. I see that my gain is good; my lamp does not go out, but it burns continually through the night, I am prepared for whatever lies ahead. I stretch out my hands to the distaff, and my hands hold the spindle as I spin wool into thread for clothing. I open and extend my hand to the poor, and I reach out my filled hands to the needy. I do not fear the snow for my household. All in my household are clothed in expensive scarlet wool. I make for myself coverlets, cushions, and rugs of tapestry. My clothing is linen, pure and fine, and purple wool. My husband is known in the city gates when he sits among the elders of the land. I make fine linen garments and sell them, supplying sashes to the merchants. Strength and dignity are my clothing, and my position is strong and secure; I smile at the future, knowing that my family and I are prepared.

I open my mouth in skillful and godly wisdom, and the teaching of kindness is on my tongue, giving counsel and instruction. I look well at how things go in my household, and I do not eat the bread of idleness. My children rise and call me blessed, happy, prosperous, and to be admired; my husband also, he praises me saying, "Many daughters have done nobly, and well with the strength of character that is steadfast in goodness, but you excel them all!" Charm and grace are deceptive and superficial beauty is vain, but a woman who fears the Lord, reverently worshipping, obeying, serving, and trusting Him with awe-filled respect, she shall be praised. I am a woman who fears the Lord. I will have the product of my hands, and my own works will praise me in the gates of the city.

31 Characteristics of A Virtuous Woman (Dakes Annotated Reference Bible)

1. Morally Perfect v. 10
2. Invaluable v. 10
3. Trustworthy v. 11
4. Inherently good and true v. 12
5. Ingenious - proficient v. 13
6. Thrifty - laborious v. 14
7. Dutiful - considerate v. 15
8. Versatile - judicious v. 16
9. Tireless - healthy v. 17
10. Joyful - efficient v. 18
11. Watchful - cautious v.18
12. Thrifty - skillful v. 19
13. Charitable - benevolent v 20
14. Generous - merciful v. 20
15. Fearless - provident v. 21
16. Clever at decorating - furnishing v. 22
17. Refined in taste v. 22
18. Respected - popular v. 23
19. Industrious - prosperous v. 24
20. Dependable - honest v. 25
21. Confident - hopeful v. 25
22. Wise - discreet v. 26

23. Kind - understanding v. 26

24. Prudent - practical v. 27

25. Energetic -ever active v. 27

26. An ideal wife and mother v. 28

27. Honored by her family v. 27-28

28. Excels in virtue v. 28

29. God-fearing - humble v. 30

30. Deserving - successful v.31

31. Honored by the public v. 31

Her husband has absolute confidence in her faithfulness and he knows she will not be one who wastes. He is blessed by her all the days of his life. He continuously praises her virtues and blessings to others. These are the benefits and the blessings of submission. Your man will brag about you to others!

I am a Proverbs 31 Woman!

(Speak it out loud and believe it.)

as he pleased, even leaving me alone all night at times. Drugs and alcohol were his recreation and was our way of a good time when we were together. Feeling alone, depressed, and unwanted brewed an anger on the inside that often expressed itself outwardly with my fists punching through walls and me kicking holes through those same walls. I wasn't afraid to fight when an argument brewed and would not stop until I felt I made my point. The fighting and the arguments were always superficial. We never addressed what the real problem was, I am not even sure we knew. What I do know is there was always conflict and not resolution. Constant conflict led to anger and anger led to depression.

Depression led to suicidal thoughts, and I was convinced my life was over. The day came when I decided to take my life. It was fueled by the thought that my marriage had ended. After yet another night of arguing, which often-times ended with James threatening to divorce me and being left alone all night into the next day, I decided to just end it all. The thoughts of my husband no longer wanting to be with me, anger and stress overwhelming me, I felt consumed with emotions that I truly did not know how to handle in a positive way. I grabbed a prescription bottle filled with my husband's anti-seizure medication and poured the small pills in my palm. I have no doubt that I had more than 50 pills. I popped all of them in my mouth at the same time and swallowed. I honestly felt nothing, however within minutes I was on the phone calling my supervisor at work, crying and telling her that I wanted to end my life and that I had taken the pills. As soon as I hung up, the police were standing at my front door. At this point, I am numb. I am no longer angry and no longer crying; no longer sad. I remember the two officers expressing concern; one defeatedly saying, "We got another one". I was rushed to the ER encouraged to drink a cup of liquid charcoal and then to IC' What still gets me today, is how my body was reacting wh

Chapter 5
My Testimony

My relationship with my husband started out like many. We were young, immature, naive, and had yet to experience life. At nineteen years of age, I decided to get married, James was eighteen. By the time we were married we had been dating for 2 years and living together for one of those years. I worked at a fast-food restaurant which eventually became our only source of income. James worked at the same restaurant which is where we met. The day we got married, I can truly say my life changed... and not for the better. Drug usage became part of my daily routine. Daily arguments and disagreements became the norm. Lonely nights with marijuana joints and cigarettes for companions were my escape. We lived paycheck to paycheck for many years because of terrible spending habits. Soon after we were married James became disabled, having seizure-like episodes, often; almost daily at one point. These 'episodes' caused a lot of strain on the relationship; he lost his job and even his license because of the danger the episodes put him in. On top of that, every time he had an episode, his attitude toward me was that of anger. Living a life of drugs, alcohol and feeling lonely sent me into a downward spiral of depression and suicidal tendencies. Communication was nearly non-existent and our sex life was literally there to satisfy sexual urges and requests (no intimacy at all). My attempts at intimacy were only there in effort to keep my husband interested. Even still adultery materialized (on both parts) which caused furth threat to the demise of our relationship.

Our relationship was not a marriage. I worked full tir kept our home clean, and did the laundry. James came and wo being monitored but I did not physically or mentally feel anything. My blood pressure was elevated, and pulse rate was extremely high; I was told it was as if I was having a seizure inwardly without outward expression. I now know that the hand of GOD Almighty was on me from the very beginning. After an overnight stay in the ICU, I was taken by police transport to the local mental facility for additional treatment. I was there less than a week, because of a good report to the doctor from my mother-in-law. It was her opinion of me that convinced the doctor to release me.

Life did not change after leaving the facility. I went back to work and to school (taking a medical assistant/phlebotomy certification class), and continued smoking weed and drinking alcohol occasionally. I did not continue the anti-depression pills prescribed to me while in the facility and did not seek any type of counseling. I just went on like nothing happened, and so did everyone else. As time went on, I continued to bury my feelings and used distraction to try and cope, however anger still raged on the inside, and I would often think of ways of how I could treat James the way I felt he was treating me. I started noticing changes in James and had the deep-down feeling that he was cheating on me. It became downright obvious, although he felt as though he was getting away undetected. I would even have dreams of him committing the act of adultery and would see a clear picture of the woman in my dreams. It was in these moments that my suspicions were further confirmed. One day he took a shower as soon as he walked through the door, after being out all day. He would take private calls on his cell phone (not allowing me to have a cell phone), deleting calls and texts. There were so many instances that he was having extra-marital affairs, but a suspicion is just that with no hard proof. However, when a woman has that gut feeling that her man is cheating, especially when she is faithful, then he is more than likely cheating. It would be years later before James decided to reveal verbally that he did in fact cheat on me multiple times.

In an act of revenge (before James' confession), I decided cheating on him would be my way of showing him that how I was being treated can go both ways. My hurt, anger, fears and frustration would no longer be one sided. That act ended quickly, when I soon realized fighting hurt with hurt only caused me further anguish and disappointment. I was truly disgusted with myself and vowed I would never deliberately hurt my husband in that way ever again. To see him hurt and so disappointed in me, made me feel even worse. Regardless of how I was being treated. Even though I vowed to never commit adultery again, I still found myself in a situation (as years passed) where I allowed myself to become emotionally attached to a man. I've learned that emotional relationships are still very unhealthy in marriages and should be avoided at all costs. For some women, an emotional relationship can be just as damaging, if not more, in our marriages.

James and I continued to spend the better part of our marriage going through the motions and doing just enough to get by. Until one day, after about 13 years of marriage, as I was seriously considering divorce, GOD Almighty Himself spoke to me. I had already made my decision to leave and nothing and no one could change my mind. At this point I was completely disgusted with James and had even confided in a friend of my decision to leave. James and I had sat down and discussed finances, child custody and support and living arrangements. I was tired and did not want to spend the next 13 years of my life playing a role. The Truth came as I was in my closet praying to my Father. James and my marriage were the furthest thing from my mind while I kneeled to pray. I was spending time with my Lord, as I had a habit of doing. However, during my conversation, telling Him my thoughts, He hit me with the following words... "He is your husband." No grandiose, aha moment or anything like that. I wasn't approached with a blinding light to get my attention or anything of the dramatic nature. It was direct but gentle and reassuring. Some would even say, that still small voice of THE LORD spoke to me right there in my closet, while I was on my knees, believing I had it all figured out. I did not question it, I did not ask Him to repeat it, and I did not ask for a sign. It was one of only a couple of times I have heard His voice audibly in my life thus far. I knew Who and what I heard wasn't me. In an instant, I felt an overwhelming peace and renewed love for my husband. I knew I was making a mistake by wanting a divorce and allowing my emotions to make decisions for me. I can truly say that this was one of those moments where the spirit of my mind had been renewed. I did not hesitate to go to James and tell him what I experienced. I also told my friend with joy and excitement, as I realized I had never felt this way about James in our entire relationship. It was in this transitional moment that my husband and I truly began to work and fight for our marriage. I loved him more now than ever and I knew it was the Spirit of GOD that changed me.

    Now I do realize, many of you may not ever have or have had The Most High come to you personally and say that your man is your husband. However, I do believe that He will place people in your life and allow certain situations to occur to show you that the man you are with is in fact your husband. I also believe that if you ask Him to show you who your husband is, or if the man you are married to, is the 'one', He will confirm it for you. Quite honestly, there are some of us who are in committed relationships with men, The Most High did not ordain for us. We get married for all the wrong reasons, then we try to stay for all the wrong reasons, then we turn around and get divorced for all the wrong reasons. Therefore it is so important to cultivate an intimate relationship with the Heavenly Father first and foremost before we become intimately involved with a man. I would not change any of my life's experiences because I know I would not be where I am today if I had not gone through them; however, I do know some things could have been avoided or at least handled differently had I been taught early on about the standards of GOD. I strongly believe in reconciliation, and I know GOD can make even the wrong marriage right when both parties are willing to work and make the lifelong commitment to love one another. Of course, I am not referring to any relationship where there is a clear conflict of religious beliefs or abuse. The Most High would not want us to be unequally yoked. When it comes to you being with someone who doesn't have any religious background, the sanctified wife sanctifies her husband and the sanctified husband sanctifies his wife, 1 Corinthians 7.14-16. Yet and still there are women who have married men that GOD did not intend for them to marry. Now I am not an advocate for divorce, nevertheless, I do believe our Heavenly Father loves us so much, He will do what is necessary to right our wrongs, fix our mistakes. In the midst of temptation, there is a way of escape. He is faithful and will always provide a way out that you may be capable, strong, and powerful enough to bear it patiently. You may have been tempted to marry out of excitement, the need to feel loved, pressure or commitment; whatever the reason, if you married a man that you know is not your husband, pray and ask GOD to help you. Then trust that He will. He is faithful to His Word.

    At the writing of this chapter, James and I have been married for exactly 20 years, fighting for our covenant relationship for the past 7 years, and still feel as though we are honeymooners! Praise GOD Almighty! My love for James grows every day. He still gives me butterflies and makes me buckle over in laughter. We have our inside jokes that are only funny to us. We share an intimacy that has drawn us closer physically and emotionally. He is my best friend, and I wouldn't change anything we have experienced. The life we have together now is the greatest thing I could have ever imagined. It didn't have to take 14 years to get here, however all things work together for good when you love GOD and are called according to His purpose. The Most High loves us and is deeply concerned about us and our well-being. When we choose to have confidence in our relationship with Him and His Word, He will always reveal His plan and purpose for our lives. I am so grateful that He spoke to me in that closet and even more grateful that I heard Him when He did. I am also grateful that James has made the commitment to serve GOD and submit to Him. Because of his commitment and desire to please The Most High, he works hard to ensure our marriage is pleasing to the LORD as well. I am grateful that he chooses to love me through all my ups and downs and together we choose to submit to GOD Almighty because He loves us.

    I failed to work on my marriage in so many ways and suffered because of it. Yours doesn't have to suffer like mine did. Your relationship does not have to take more than a decade to be what The Most High designed it to be. Whether you have just gotten married, been married for 20 or 40 years, or just getting ready to jump the broom, please know that your covenant union can and should be one that models the plan of our Heavenly Father. Submission is an important factor to that plan. I strongly believe that my relationship with The Most High and my submission to Him, was the difference between getting a divorce and choosing to stay in my marriage. I could have easily said 'no' when I heard the voice of The LORD tell me that James was my husband. My yes, your yes, is the difference between life and death. The "yes" will be hard work and it will be a challenge to fight every day, but it is worth it. The opposite is so much worse and honestly, in my opinion, the fight is so mentally draining that you won't have the energy for it anyway. The choice to say no is an uphill battle that never ends. That's why it took me over 10 years to get it right. I was fighting for so long saying 'no' to my marriage when all along the LORD wanted me to look to Him and say yes to His way. It basically comes down to the same truth Joshua brought to the children of Israel in Joshua chapter 24, choose this day whom you will serve: some other god or the LORD. Choosing the LORD is choosing submission which brings life. Jesus Christ came to bring us life and life more abundantly. How else do we partake of the abundant life without first choosing to make Him LORD of our lives?

I will admit that my marriage was not ideal in the beginning. James and I had many valid reasons to call it quits and get a divorce. There was physical, mental, sexual, and drug abuse for many years. It was only by the grace of GOD Almighty that we made it through those years and are even still alive today. In fact, I do believe that if we were to go back in time, I probably would not have gotten married.

Choosing to give my life to Jesus Christ wholeheartedly has had a major impact on the transformation in my marriage relationship and how I view submission. Submission is not a burden, it is very liberating. I no longer must worry or be afraid. I know now when I submit to GOD, it makes it easier to submit to my husband and my relationship.

Chapter 6
It Brings Rest and Peace

As a woman chooses to submit to her husband, she will find rest and peace in every situation... Eventually. Being submissive can be one of the most challenging aspects of any relationship, even the more with your spouse. Especially when the act of submissiveness comes at a time when we must give our husbands the lead. Every. Single. Time. It may not even be an issue of giving him the lead but also knowing that the decision he is making is a huge mistake. Or the route he chooses to take us is completely opposite of where we need to go. There are times when you may find yourself at the short end of the stick, especially in heated situations and circumstances. You know the right way to take, the best decision to make, the "better" way to handle it, however the man of the house has the final say and his decision is just as final. I can remember multiple occasions where James decided that I honestly knew should have been different. However, I wanted him to feel and know that his opinion mattered, and he had the right to do things his way. All the while, deep down I'm cringing on the inside because I know at the end of this terrible decision HE is making, WE are going to have to figure a way out of it. It happened every time. Every. Single. Time. Something had to change. So how do we handle this? How could I possibly allow my husband to make such terrible decisions? Decisions that affect not only him but the entire household. It's easy, sort of!

    This is when effective prayer becomes an especially important aspect to add to our daily lives. As godly wives, we need to allow our husbands to lead. Husbands are the head of wives, just as Christ is the Head of the church. Allowing our husbands to lead the household is one of the greatest acts of respect we can show. Yes, even when WE know the decision, he is making is not ideal. Men know when they have made a mistake and don't need us women to remind them of how bad they messed up. Oftentimes, he makes the mistake and you both must clean it up! The prayer is that he learned from the mistake and chooses more wisely the next time. Also, when you've given him the space to make the decision without ridicule and in turn be there for him when he may fail, he will be more likely to include you and your opinion the next time. Your effective prayer is the necessary step to take to ensure change in this area. Pray for the heart and mindset of your husband and expect GOD to come through for you. HE will answer your prayers and you will be well on your way to making decisions *with* your husband instead of just cleaning up behind them. In the event your husband does mess up, be ready with an encouraging attitude to help, not with a 'matter - of - fact' or "I told you so" demeanor. Husbands want to be heroes and want to *feel* that way as well. They want their wives to appreciate what they do, even if the act seems small in your eyes. They want to be able to protect their household and be acknowledged for the work done. When we respect our husbands' position and his decisions, he feels empowered and loved. In a world where men are already viewed as aggressive, sexist, and lacking compassion, it's important for men to come home and feel safe. Safe enough to make decisions without ridicule or pessimism. As wives, we hold a great amount of power in the success of our husbands outside the home. When your husband feels confident at home, he will be confident outside the home. When he feels encouraged to be a great provider and protector, he will feel encouraged to do great at his workplace, at home, and in the world.

    Like women, men need affection, affirmation, and acceptance. Our husbands will not get this in the world. We need to be in position, as submissive wives, to be our husband's best friends and closest companions. The moment we fail in any of these areas of our marriage, especially for an extended period, it gives opportunity for the enemy to step in and temptation immediately follows. We do not ever want to find ourselves in a situation where our husbands find affection, affirmation, or acceptance from an outside source (another woman, pornography, work, etc.). It only takes a moment for the right words to be spoken during a time of vulnerability for a man to fall prey to the enticement of another woman. It doesn't even have to be sexual in nature. Just like us women, if a man is lacking in his relationship and another comes along offering what is missing, sometimes it can be a challenge to resist the temptation if that man is not resolute in his marriage covenant. The resistance can be even more of a challenge if the relationship is not already set on a firm foundation of trust, love, respect, and submission.

Temptation breeds lust and lust gives birth to sin. When sin enters your covenant relationship, it will bring storms. Being unsubmissive in marriage is like standing in the rain during the storm with a hole in your umbrella. The covering is there but you are still getting wet. You have what you need to protect you from the elements, however it is ineffective in its position. When the husband is ineffective in his position as head of the household, as the covering, you have a home that will eventually fall apart. This is not to say that storms will not come or that you won't get caught in the rain without an umbrella. However, when we choose to live submissive roles in our covenant relationships, we can withstand the storm together, being sheltered from the storm with GOD Most High as our Covering. There are certain storms that as married couples we should never have to encounter, however there are some storms that are most certainly unavoidable. We need to be prepared for both. This is where our personal relationships with The Creator become very vital to our spiritual and emotional health and well-being.

We all know about the storms of life by just living in the world. We experience the deaths of people we love, sickness and disease, stress, depression, financial hardships and so much more. However, the storms we should never have to experience, especially in our covenant relationships, are infidelity, adultery, deception, hatred, the lack of love, and respect. Unfortunately, because so many have experienced and dealt with these things, it has almost been accepted and regarded as understandable behavior. This is where our personal relationships with GOD Almighty should really show evident in our personal lives. As a Believer, my priority should be to please Him and with that, whatever is unacceptable to Him, should be unacceptable to me. Just because so many couples have experienced the pain of adultery and deception does not mean it should be accepted as something that "just happens." The flip side of that is the fact that because it has been accepted as "understandable" in our society, we should do well by preparing ourselves. Now I am not saying, live your life with a mindset that your spouse is going to cheat (or lie) on you at some point or even have it in the back of your mind. When I say prepare, I mean taking the time to truly get to know the one you are marrying/married to. Be always aware and pray for wisdom and direction. GOD Almighty will show you the signs. Most of the time when a man is cheating on his wife, the wife knows deep down that it is happening. She may not have solid, concrete proof and may not have seen him in the act, but she knows. Some call it women's intuition. I choose to believe that it is the Spirit of GOD within us, letting us know that something is not right. Nothing will ever prepare a woman's heart to handle the pain of adultery, deception, or hatred from their man. It is one of the most painful things in the world; anyone that has had this experience knows exactly what I am talking about. It is this type of hurt, pain, and rejection that we must know how to depend on GOD to get through. We never have expectations to go through trials, but it is so much easier to handle when we know we have the tools, knowledge, and support to utilize when they come.

We should not be ignorant of any of the strategies and devices of the enemy; and he has a lot of them. He will use every trick, plot, plan, and then some to get you to fall to his demise. He has been using the same tactics for years, and they work, so don't think he is going to change or do something special for you. Whatever can be used to separate you from being on one accord with your husband, he will try to tempt you with it. If you already have a strained relationship because of finances, here comes an unexpected repair bill. The devil will use that strain and plant a seed of doubt to make you believe that you will never get out of debt. Financial struggles are hard all by themselves, we do not need a pessimistic view added to the mix. But the devil can and will use that to get you off your game. Finances are one of the biggest reasons people get divorced these days. But we are talking about submission here so we will move on. The point is, do not open the door and invite the enemy in for tea and biscuits when you are working to be totally submissive in your relationship.

Preparing your heart and mind through prayer, praying the Scriptures specifically, will equip you to handle every road you may face. First Corinthians chapter 10 verse 13 tells us that temptations in our life are no different from what others experience. GOD Almighty is faithful and will not allow any temptation to be more than you can stand. With every temptation He will show you a way out so that you can endure. So regardless of what life may bring, GOD Almighty is right there to help you endure and overcome. Rest and peace are your portion. It is always available and is promised in a life totally surrendered to Jesus Christ. Jesus said in Matthew chapter 11, "Come to Me, all of you who are weary and carry heavy burdens, and I will give you rest. Take My yoke upon you. Let Me teach you, because I am humble and gentle at heart, and you will find rest for your souls. For My yoke is easy to bear, and the burden I give you is light." (NLT) He also said in the book of John 14 verse 27, "I am leaving you with a gift - peace of mind and heart. And the peace I give is a gift the world cannot give. So don't be troubled or afraid."

When we choose to do it GOD's way it is so much easier. We truly don't have to stress or worry about our marriages or our spouses. We can take comfort in knowing that when we submit to Him, He is in control and going to take care of everything. If you have never given it all to HIM before or are new to doing it, yes it can be a challenge at first, but it gets easier. Over time, as you see HIM work things out for your best interest, your faith will build. As your faith increases you begin to experience the rest and peace that only comes from a life of servitude to The Most High.

So, I am choosing to be submissive to my husband today. I am thankful for my home, so I clean it daily. I am grateful to have a running vehicle, so I wash it and get it serviced regularly. My children are a blessing from GOD Almighty; I love them, take care of them, and ensure they have all they need to be healthy, strong, and happy. I have placed value in my home because it gives me shelter. I have placed value in my vehicle because it takes me where I need to go, and it is a very necessary asset for me and my family. My children are invaluable to me, and I will go to great lengths to ensure their wellbeing. I choose to love them and train them to be honest, respectful and individuals of integrity. I also chose to get married and commit to be with my husband till death. To love and cherish him through sickness and health. How could I not be grateful for my husband who promised to do the same for me? So how much value do I place in my relationship with my spouse? What actions are taken to show that I do value and care for him?

Being ungrateful opens the door to vain imaginations. It also puts you in a head space that welcomes the enemy to come in and reside. It literally only takes one negative thought to spiral out of control and take you to a place you never intended to be. Now these vain imaginations are not the ones where you are always thinking about how beautiful you are and being prideful; or being conceited about how you look or how well you do certain things. However, I am referring to those useless thoughts that lead to nowhere but downfall and destruction. The futile thinking patterns. In the scripture reference Romans 1.21-25, Paul is speaking to Roman Christians about a world that has lost respect and reverence for the Creator. Going so far as to worship men, birds, and animals. This type of thinking was futile and today the same still holds true. We still have these same practices going on in the world today. This choice to worship the created thing instead of the Creator led to vain imaginations, which in turn caused these same people to turn to ungodly and indecent behaviors. Eventually the people were "filled (permeated and saturated) with every kind of unrighteousness, iniquity, grasping and covetous greed, and malice. They were full of envy and jealousy, murder, strife, deceit and treachery, ill will, and cruel ways. They were secret backbiters and gossipers," and so much more. Romans 1.29 (AMPC)

    What drives us as a people to choose to worship 'things' in our lives? Romans chapter 1 makes it clear there is no true value in worshipping creation. That in fact doing so, leads us to destruction. Something in life caused the people in this world to become ungrateful and no longer feel the necessity to glorify the Almighty. We find this time after time with the children of Israel after their exodus from Pharaoh in Egypt. Even after experiencing such miraculous events (that are beyond comprehension), they would quickly forget what GOD Almighty had done for them and begin complaining about what they did not have. The Red Sea was parted for them to walk on dry ground and escape the hands of their previous oppressors in Exodus chapter 14 and in the very next chapter, the people complained about not having water to drink and no food to eat in chapter 16. Now why would a God that literally made a way out of no way to save your life, not provide food and water to preserve that very same life!

However, this is how we are as a people. We experience great and awesome things. Absolutely wonderful circumstances happen for us, but the moment we get a kink in the flow, we immediately forget everything good and now everything is ALL BAD. So, what happens to cause us to choose the created thing rather than the Creator. Maybe it is because there are not many miracles, if not any at all, being seen. Perhaps we feel it's just more fun to do whatever each one pleases -whether it is right or wrong. Maybe it is because we just need to have a tangible substance that we can grasp with our hands and our minds so we can feel as though we are connected to something bigger than us. Whatever the reason, in this first chapter of Romans and in our society today, the world chose to no longer give thanks to GOD Almighty. They stopped glorifying Him which ultimately equates to no longer submitting to Him. But everyone knows and knows even now, who He is. They know of His role and His many miracles. What is to be known about God has been made plain; "for since the creation of the world, God's invisible qualities - His eternal power and divine nature have been clearly seen" by all. Therefore, there is no excuse. Romans 1.20

As a wife, if you are choosing to not submit to your husband it is because of a specific reason. And it is much deeper than feeling like you don't want to be controlled.

****side note*** I am not referring to abusive relationships. If you are reading this book or have stumbled upon this chapter and you are a victim of an abusive relationship, do whatever you can to seek help from someone you trust or an organization and GET OUT SAFELY. This goes for verbal, physical, and emotional abuse. GOD Almighty would never want to see His beautiful daughters being treated any less than the royal creations He designed them to be. So please do not get stuck in a place where you feel you are biblically obligated to stay in an abusive situation. And if ANY MAN (or woman) is telling you to stay in an abusive relationship because 'GOD hates divorce', then they are part of the problem, and you should look elsewhere for sound advice and wisdom. ***

Now back to all of us who are married or looking to be married to these decent, hard- headed, know-it-all, assertive, courageous men who we love dearly and would also love to punch just as passionately. Submission in marriage is critical. When we don't submit, it is because we made the choice not to do so. Devoted Believers respect GOD Almighty, and because of that respect we choose to follow His commands and do what He says. Jesus Christ said if you love me, do what I command. We do our best to walk in righteousness and holiness. We don't go around willfully sinning, and if we do make a mistake, with sincere hearts, from a posture of humility, we ask for forgiveness and repent. That is the goal and the life of a submitted Believer of Jesus Christ. We understand the work done at the Cross and we have placed great value in our faith and how we choose to believe. That choice causes Believers all around the world to submit to GOD Almighty and resist the devil. The Bible is our law, and we abide by that law wholeheartedly. The Word of GOD is invaluable and nothing and no one can replace it. As Believers of Jesus Christ, we also understand there are consequences when we choose to disobey the Word and do things our own way. For example, the world may say love those that love you, however the Word teaches to love everyone, even your enemies; to pray for those that persecute you. Jesus said that if you deny Him before others, He will deny you before the Father, but if you acknowledge Him, He will acknowledge you. In other words, love Him regardless of what others think or what others may say, and likewise He will do the same.

So, what does all of this have to do with submission? It's simple really. If you say you love GOD Almighty and are deeply committed to Him, then there is no problem submitting to Him and His authority. His supreme reign over you is just that, supreme and you are okay with that. With that, then you also understand that if you choose to not submit and commit to Him and His Word then you will suffer the consequences. We understand GOD Almighty is holy and His standards deserve more than subpar obedience. Half obedience is disobedience. When we put the standards of our relationship with The Most High against the subject of our marriage relationships, we should put the same amount of effort, reverence, love and commitment. We choose to get married and therefore must choose to love our husbands and respect them as such. Ephesians 5.22 tells wives to submit to their own husbands as you do to the Lord. Going on to say that us wives need to submit to our husbands in EVERYTHING. So, what happens when we choose to not submit to our husbands. There are many reasons I am sure, however what reason is good enough to forgo the blessings and benefits gained from a submissive relationship? Whatever your reason, go to the LORD and His Word and compare it to His standard. What does He say? What does the Bible say? If your reason for not submitting is because you feel your husband is not holy enough, what does the Bible tell you to do on how to handle the situation? Is your reason because he doesn't talk to you, he is controlling, demanding, rude, a know-it-all? The Bible has an answer to it all (and no, it is not to handle everything by yourself because you can do it better)! There is one Scripture that can sum it all up and cover every single reason you have. I bet you are asking, which verse is that? I thought you'd never ask! Ephesians 6 verse 18 "With all prayer and petition, pray with specific requests at all times on every occasion and in every season in the Spirit, and with this in view, stay alert with all perseverance and petition interceding in prayer for all GOD's people." AMP

Your husband is included in "all GOD's people." We must pray for our situations and our husbands. This is a vital part of a submissive life. Pray about everything.

Another verse we can rely on through any situation and reason is first Thessalonians 5.15-18 "See that no one repays another with evil for evil, but always seek that which is good for one another and for all people. Rejoice always and delight in your faith; be unceasing and persistent in prayer; in every situation no matter what the circumstances be thankful and continually give thanks to GOD; for this is the will of GOD for you in Christ Jesus." It is GOD Almighty's will for your life to rejoice *for* everything, pray *about* everything, be grateful *in* everything, and give *thanks* no matter the situation. When you take the bold letters in the last sentence and put them together, they spell *faith.* Faith is key to fulfilling HIS will for you. Put your full confidence in His Word. Trust Him, trust the process, take joy in the rest you find, and the joy you will experience. It's like nothing you have ever felt before.

Your reasons to not submit to your husband may be valid and you have every right to feel loved, respected, and appreciated. However, when you feel you are not getting these needs met, this fulfillment must come from God. When you feel you are not being loved, you must know that God loves you first. When you may feel like your husband is not respecting your opinions or your place as his wife, you must find peace in God to overcome these emotions. It is not until God is sustaining you in every area will you be better equipped to handle the reactions of your husband and respond in a way that honors God and is submissive. This will bring peace in knowing that, regardless of how your husband may not be fulfilling his role, **you** are still doing what you need to do to be pleasing to God. If your only task on this earth was to be a godly wife, and I am not saying that it is, just go with me for a moment; what excuse would you really bring before The Most High as he evaluates your life and questions you on whether you did a job well done? You see, at the end of the day, it's you and GOD. He is worth more than our reasons and our excuses. It is only in Him that we truly find rest and peace, for our souls and for our marriages.

Chapter 7
Prayer for Self And Spouse

Trust in the LORD with all your heart and lean not on your own understanding; in all your ways acknowledge Him, and He shall direct your paths. Do not be wise in your own eyes; Fear the LORD and depart from evil. It will be health to your flesh, and strength to your bones. Proverbs 3:5 NKJV

I strongly believe prayer is one of the most powerful things we can do in our lives. We go through so much, and oftentimes find ourselves in situations that we cannot see the way out. Prayer is the way out! When we choose to pray instead of argue, fight, hide, cower, or shut down, we give The Most High an opportunity to step in and do what only He can do. The key to effective prayer is to pray His Holy Scriptures. The Lord GOD Almighty told Jeremiah in chapter 1 that He was watching to see that His Word was fulfilled. Declare and decree His Word and it shall be established (Job 22.28a) in your situation and He will watch over that same Word to see it come to pass for YOU! Come to The Lord with a pure and clean heart (mind). Choose to forgive, let go of the bitterness, anger, fear and resentment and allow The GOD of Peace to lead your heart into true prayer with Him. The following prayer, inspired by Scripture, can help you. I suggest you have your Bible in hand while you pray, in the event The Most High places a Scripture in your heart. It's okay to stop and read a Scripture and then pick up where you left off. The Most High may even lead you to pray for your husband in a completely different way. Pray often, in unwavering faith, and watch GOD Almighty work!

Heavenly Father, I come to You in the mighty name of Jesus Christ; lead me by Your Holy Spirit. I first ask for forgiveness of all sins, debts, trespasses and every evil work that is in my life. I repent to you now for all the anger, fear, unforgiveness, bitterness, selfishness, and resentment that may be operating in my life. I know that You did not give me a spirit of fear but a spirit of power, love, and a sound mind. Your perfect love casts out all fear. I understand I must walk in forgiveness so that I may be forgiven by You. Jesus thank you for dying on the cross for me, so that I may be forgiven. Thank You for taking all my sins away and not holding them against me as I pray.

My Heavenly Father, I lift my husband up to You now. I release him completely to You and I thank You for taking him and lifting him in Your Righteous Right Hand. Cover _____ with the precious Blood of Jesus and anoint him with Your Presence. Fill him with Your presence that he may honor You in everything he does. Bless him in every area of his life and open his eyes to see and acknowledge Your wonderful presence in every area of his life. I pray that _____ will always be a man of integrity in word and in deed. His every action of work will be to glorify You in Heaven and not man.

I declare and decree that his mind will be renewed daily. He will lead every thought and purpose captive and into the obedience of Christ. He will choose to refute every argument and every proud and lofty thing that sets itself up against the true knowledge of You, GOD Most High.

Every relationship he has will be holy and godly according to Your standards and not his own. In every temptation, he will not be overtaken and will see the way of escape so that he can bear it and walk in victory over sin, for You are a faithful GOD. I trust him to make godly decisions concerning his personal life, our relationship, and our family. When he makes a mistake, I pray he will be quick to repent and get back in right standing with You. I believe by faith, he will not allow mistakes, failures, or hurts (past, present, or future) to hinder him from moving forward into his GOD-given purpose.

His reputation will be one of honesty, holiness, and righteousness. Teach him how to give You his fears, doubts, and concerns, not giving into his own understanding but acknowledging You in all things, so that You can direct him in every way.

Bless his heart, brain, stomach, and every organ in his body. I pray for a strong immune system that will fight off sickness, illness, and disease in the way You designed his body to operate. Any sickness or infirmity that may be present now or may come, I rebuke and bind it now in the name of Jesus. The blood of Jesus Christ covers his entire being right now to bring forth healing and deliverance; I loose the blood now into his atmosphere and his temple. No weapon formed against him will prosper. He is healed, delivered, and set free from every form of bondage that would attempt to attach to or attack his body. I bind all heart disease, high blood pressure, diabetes and every other illness and command them GO! I loose Your healing virtue and Your power over him now. Thank You LORD GOD Almighty for healing him. Remove all doubt and fear that would cause me to not trust You in this area and all areas of his life.

Thank You LORD for teaching him how to prioritize perfectly and properly; keeping You first and foremost, how to keep me, as his wife, before children, work, and activities. And I will do the same in my life, GOD first, and he as my husband, before children, work, and activities. _____ is an excellent father, meeting the emotional, spiritual, and physical needs of our children. Teaching and showing our children, as head of the household, how to be practical, responsible, and respectful individuals. He will not exasperate our children but will bring them up in the training and instruction of the LORD.

I pray that his attitude is one that reflects the nature and character of Christ. The Fruit of the Spirit is evident and operational in every area, being a good tree that bears good fruit. Teach him to have unwavering faith, to walk in obedience to Your Word, and to see himself exactly as You see him - forgiven, loved, strong, wanted and needed.

He will be submissive out of reverence to Christ. He will love me, as his wife, just as Christ loves the church and gave Himself for it. He loves himself and will therefore love me as his own body, and I will always respect him.

_____ is my husband and You chose him just for me. Our covenant relationship will reflect the godly marriage You ordained for us to have. We have the power and authority, in the name of Jesus Christ, to trample every serpent and scorpion that would attempt to come against our marriage. We will choose to love one another regardless of situations, circumstances, and people. We will seek only godly wisdom and will quickly remove all hindrances and nay-sayers that would speak negative things into our covenant. We choose to uplift each other and not tear each down with our thoughts, words, and actions. We will encourage one another and focus on the good, not the negative and the failures. A righteous man may fall seven times, but he will get back up. I will be there to pick my husband up when he falls, and he will be here to pick me up when I fall. Thank You LORD for being part of our three-banded cord that is not easily broken. We will stand together to resist every enemy that would attempt to break our union. In Jesus Name!

I love you Heavenly Father, Jesus Christ, Holy Spirit. Thank You for hearing my prayer as I cry out to You. I thank you in advance for answering my prayers and moving on behalf of me and my husband in this season of our lives. I am grateful for all you have done and all that you are doing for us. I now humble myself to hear your voice. Speak to my heart. I am listening. Amen.

(Allow a few moments of quiet time and listen for the voice of Father GOD Almighty to speak to your heart. He may give you a scripture verse, a word, or you may not hear anything.

Even if you don't hear anything, giving pause to give Him an opportunity to speak is a part of prayer. Remember prayer is a conversation! Listen for that still small voice.)

About the Author

LaShawna Thomas is currently the Co-Pastor of House of HIS Dwelling Ministers in Stone Mountain, Georgia, where she where she serves with her supportive and loving husband of 20 years, James. Together, they have 5 children and reside in Rockdale County, Georgia. She loves spending time in prayer, family time, watching movies, listening to music, writing, journaling, nature, and going to the beach. GOD MOST HIGH is definitely her first love and strives every day to please Him, keep Him first, and following His lead. HIS presence is her happy place. She believes in cultivating quality relationships that will bring restoration and renewal to our spirit-man to walk out our GOD-given purpose. The first relationship that must be cultivated is with our Heavenly Father. When we get to know Him and our identity in Him, then we can understand our reason for living.

Connect with me!

Email: houseofhisdwelling@gmail.com

Facebook: LaShawna Thomas

Instagram: @houseofhisdwelling_ Kingdom Work

www.ingramcontent.com/pod-product-compliance
Lightning Source LLC
Chambersburg PA
CBHW072102290426
44110CB00014B/1792